NOW!⚡
CLASSROOMS
LEADER'S GUIDE

ENHANCING TEACHING
AND LEARNING
THROUGH TECHNOLOGY

MEG ORMISTON

Cathy Fisher   **Courtney Orzel**   **Robin Bruebach**
Jamie Reilly   **Jordan Garrett**   **Steven M. Griesbach**
Becky Fischer

Solution Tree | **Press**
a division of
Solution Tree

555 North Morton Street
Bloomington, IN 47404
800.733.6786 (toll free) / 812.336.7700
FAX: 812.336.7790

email: info@SolutionTree.com
SolutionTree.com

Visit **go.SolutionTree.com/technology** to download the free reproducibles in this book.

Printed in the United States of America

21   20   19   18   17   1   2   3   4   5

Library of Congress Cataloging-in-Publication Data

Names: Ormiston, Meghan J., author.

Title: NOW classrooms, leader's guide : enhancing teaching and learning through technology / Meg Ormiston, Cathy Fisher, Jamie Reilly, Courtney Orzel, Jordan Garrett, Robin Bruebach, Steven M. Griesbach, and Becky Fischer.

Description: Bloomington, IN : Solution Tree Press, 2018. | Series: NOW classrooms | Includes bibliographical references and index.

Identifiers: LCCN 2017020331 | ISBN 9781945349461 (perfect bound)

Subjects: LCSH: Educational change. | Education--Aims and objectives. | Educational technology. | Education--Effect of technological innovations on. | Effective teaching.

Classification: LCC LB2806 .O687 2018 | DDC 371.33--dc23 LC record available at https://lccn.loc.gov/2017020331

Solution Tree

Jeffrey C. Jones, CEO
Edmund M. Ackerman, President

Solution Tree Press

President and Publisher: Douglas M. Rife
Editorial Director: Sarah Payne-Mills
Art Director: Rian Anderson
Managing Production Editor: Caroline Cascio
Senior Editor: Amy Rubenstein
Proofreader: Kendra Slayton
Cover Designer: Rian Anderson
Editorial Assistants: Jessi Finn and Kendra Slayton

Acknowledgments

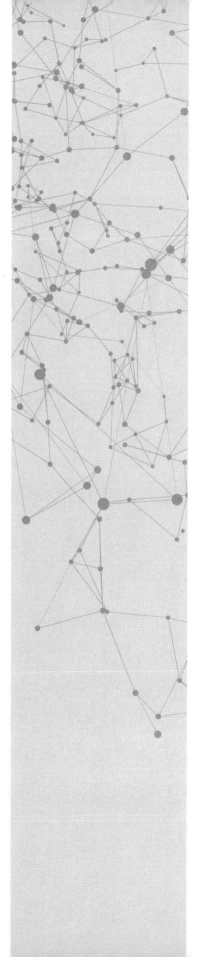

Thank you to all teachers everywhere! I am proud to say I am a teacher, and I believe it is one of the most important professions in the world. Specifically, I want to thank the collaborative writing team that coauthored this series of five books. I have never worked with a more dedicated, fun-loving, collaborative team of lifelong learners. Thanks to the Otus team for your support and to my family for putting up with our writing marathons. I give my deepest thanks to Douglas Rife and the entire team at Solution Tree for helping all of us craft this dream into a reality. Wow!

—Meg Ormiston

Special thanks to Meg Ormiston for bringing together this amazing group of educators and for providing the guidance and encouragement necessary to achieve our goal of producing five books. I am grateful to all the professionals I've met through this journey and look forward to many more collaborations.

—Cathy Fisher

A huge thank you to Meg Ormiston who caused a seismic shift in my thinking around what is possible in learning innovations. I am very thankful for my tech-savvy husband's support of my personal learning as well as that of my colleague and friend, Cathy Fisher, who always encourages me to learn more. Many kudos to the learning and technology integration coaches in Maercker School District 60 whose vision helped create learning environments that were much more conducive to engaged learning!

—Jamie Reilly

A huge thanks to Meg Ormiston for being a pioneer in the field of education and for helping me not only as a teacher but now as a superintendent.

—Courtney Orzel

To the leadership team that wrote this book—between conversations, phone calls, and emails, you have pushed my thinking more than you know. It was a pleasure to work with you all!

—Jordan Garrett

I would like to acknowledge my family for their love and support and my first-grade teacher, Mrs. Houser, who helped me believe I could do anything.

—Robin Bruebach

To everyone who inspired me to think, who challenged my views, who held me accountable, and who supported my growth as a leader and person. You cared enough to help me become my best.

—Steve Griesbach

Thank you to all the professionals who continually inspire me and to the students who drive me to work hard on their behalf every day.

—Becky Fischer

Solution Tree Press would like to thank the following reviewers:

Nikolas Gonzales
Digital Learning Specialist
Boston Public Schools
Boston, Massachusetts

Susan Herder
Instructional Technology Coordinator
Mounds View Public Schools
Arden Hills, Minnesota

Chris Larsen
Director of Educational Technology
Granite School District
Salt Lake City, Utah

Tina Lauer
Instructional Technology Specialist
City of St. Charles School District
St. Charles, Missouri

Michael Mades
Director of Technology
Sun Prairie Area School District
Sun Prairie, Wisconsin

Orly Rachamim
Director of Educational Technology
Netivot HaTorah Day School
Toronto, Ontario
Canada

Heather Shannon
Technology Integration Support Specialist
Elk Grove Unified School District
Elk Grove, California

Visit **go.SolutionTree.com/technology** to download the free reproducibles in this book.

Table of Contents

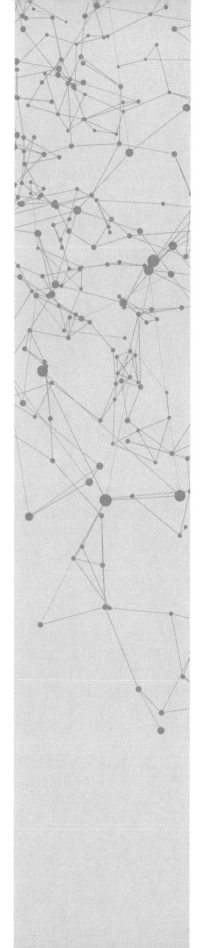

About the Authors

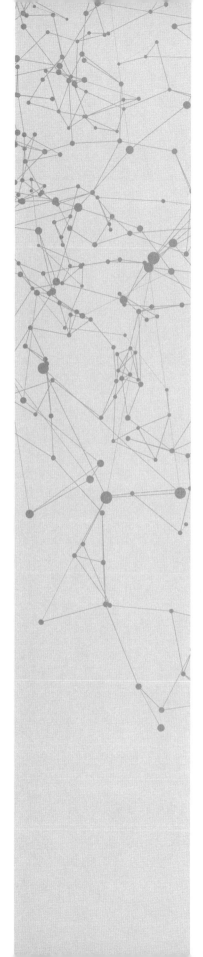

Meg Ormiston is on a mission to change the world of education. She shares her passion for teaching and learning with technology through her keynote speaking, through her writing, and on social media. Meg was a classroom teacher for twelve years and now travels nationally and internationally, speaking about the power of teaching and learning with digital tools. When Meg is home in the Chicago suburbs, you will often find her in classrooms serving as an instructional coach.

In her role as a consultant, Meg partners with school systems that are committed to 21st century learning experiences for everyone. Meg creates a unique partnership in each district, reflecting the mission, vision, and direction that local leaders have identified. Her districtwide projects have included guiding teams through the visioning process, designing and delivering professional development, facilitating classroom modeling, developing student leaders in technology, and educating parents.

As a thought leader in education technology, Meg has published seven books and is collaborating with a team for the five books in the *NOW Classrooms* series. Meg holds a master's degree in curriculum and instruction from National Louis University.

To learn more about Meg's work, follow @megormi on Twitter.

Cathy Fisher is the director of teaching and learning at Maercker School District 60 and provides leadership to all aspects of its K–8 instructional program. She is a former middle school special education teacher, dean of students, and professional development coordinator who believes strongly in continuous improvement and enjoys leading systems change.

During the district's technology integration journey, Cathy sought to expand her personal learning network, and she has been fortunate to learn from and with the authors of this book. As a former special education teacher, Cathy views herself as a student advocate, and she strives to provide the leadership necessary for schools to meet the needs of all learners.

Cathy earned a bachelor of arts in special education from Elmhurst College and a master's degree in educational leadership from National Louis University. She lives in a Chicago suburb with her husband, Matt, and her two children, Colleen and Lucas.

Jamie Reilly is a retired teacher and administrator who consults with the Consortium for Educational Change, where she continues her own learning while serving other educators.

Jamie served public school districts in both Illinois and Pennsylvania for over forty years; twenty-six as a teacher and sixteen as an administrator. Her experience includes classroom teaching at elementary grades, as well as working as a reading specialist and a trained Reading Recovery teacher. Jamie found her extensive teaching background to be helpful as she transitioned to an elementary principal, assistant superintendent for learning, and ultimately superintendent. Jamie's focus has always been continuous improvement with a personal goal to remain "green and growing."

She completed a bachelor of arts degree in education at Westminster College in Pennsylvania. Jamie's graduate studies include a doctorate in curriculum and instruction from

Aurora University, a certification in educational leadership, a master's degree from Penn State University, and advanced study at National Louis University. Jamie lives in the suburbs of Chicago with her husband, Kevin, and loves spending time with her children Carley and Robert and her precious granddaughter Maddie.

 **Courtney Orzel** serves as an elementary school superintendent in the suburbs of Chicago. She is a former principal, middle school teacher, and high school teacher. Courtney's educational interests are focused on continuous improvement models, principal and teacher leadership, dialogue, and issues of equity and access in schools.

Courtney earned her doctorate from the University of Illinois at Urbana–Champaign and her master's degree from Concordia University. She resides in the suburbs of Chicago with her husband and two children.

 **Jordan Garrett** is the iDirector (instructional director) for Berwyn South School District 100. She oversees 1:1 deployment, district iCoaches, site visits, the district's iEngage Conference, and the Students Involved in Technology (SIT) Conference. She joined the district in 2010 as a first-grade co-teacher, eventually taught fourth grade, and then became one of the district's iCoaches, traveling throughout the district to instruct and coach staff on the use, applications, and capacity of technology in the classroom. She was selected as a member of the Apple Distinguished Educator class of 2017.

Jordan has a bachelor of arts degree in elementary and special education from Butler University and a master's degree in curriculum studies from DePaul University. She loves her family, Chicago, and her fiancé Matt unconditionally.

Robin Bruebach is a principal in a K–6 building in Downers Grove School District 58. A former teacher, curriculum director, and assistant principal, Robin worked with gifted students, remedial reading students, fifth-grade students, and eighth-grade students. She coached basketball, cheerleading, and Odyssey of the Mind. Her passion is working with teachers, students, parents, and administrators through collaboration, differentiated instruction, and professional development. She is interested in developing growth mindsets and facilitating ownership of learning for all community members.

Robin earned her bachelor's degree from the University of Illinois at Urbana–Champaign and a master's degree in education from National Louis University. She loves to travel and has gained a global perspective that helps her understand the many cultures in her school. She loves sports and music and resides in a suburb of Chicago with her husband, daughter, and Goldendoodle Max.

To learn more about Robin's work, follow @ITMrsBruebach on Twitter.

Steven M. Griesbach is a retired teacher and administrator who works with superintendents and principals and consults in the EdTech world. Steve served students, families, and staff at all grade levels in public schools in Illinois, first as a high school history and social sciences teacher and later as a middle school assistant principal, elementary school principal, assistant superintendent for curriculum and instruction, and superintendent of an award-winning school district in a suburb of Chicago. Along the way, Steve learned that his primary role as an educator was to bring out the best in those he served.

Becky Fischer is the director of curriculum, instruction, and assessment at Skokie School District 73 ½. A former middle school science teacher, department chair, and sixth-grade team leader, Becky began her administrative journey as a science curriculum coordinator and then served as a middle school assistant principal. As a district leader, she derives great learning and joy from leading the district through its initial stages of adopting instructional technology with an aim toward providing staff with meaningful opportunities to understand change and the part technology tools play in teaching and learning.

Through varied professional learning opportunities, including a thoughtfully developed districtwide professional learning plan and intentional instructional coaching program, she hopes to see teachers and students continue to learn and grow. Becky's professional interests include differentiated professional learning and the power of instructional coaching.

Becky earned her bachelor's degree from Augustana College, her master's degree in curriculum from University of Phoenix, and her certificate of advanced study in educational leadership from National Louis University. Becky resides in the suburbs of Chicago with her fiancé and two dogs. She enjoys trying new restaurants, being outdoors, and running.

To book Meg Ormiston, Cathy Fisher, Jamie Reilly, Courtney Orzel, Jordan Garrett, Robin Bruebach, Steven M. Griesbach, or Becky Fischer for professional development, contact pd@SolutionTree.com.

Preface

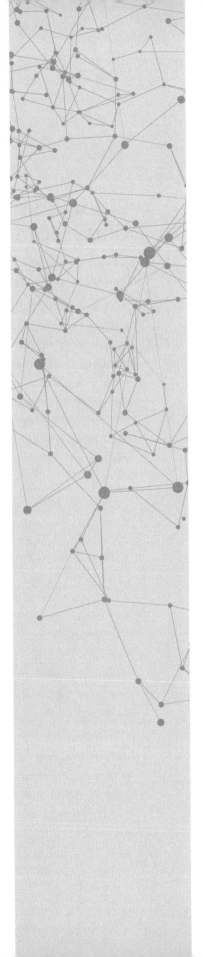

This book is all about leading a change-focused school. Each member of this writing team is a practicing school or district administrator or education consultant, and although our journeys have been different, we all share a passion for thinking about how to launch students into the rapidly changing world outside of school, equipping them with the digital skills to be lifelong learners and change agents. We also share a passion for thinking about the best practices for you—a K–12 administrator who shares these goals—to help your team create the highly engaged and digitally enriched 21st century classrooms that will lead students to develop those skills. It's with that passion that we wrote this guide for you.

We are in an *age of acceleration*, according to celebrated *New York Times* columnist and best-selling author Thomas L. Friedman. In his groundbreaking book *Thank You for Being Late*, Friedman (2016) writes, "There are vintage years in wine and vintage years in history, and 2007 was definitely one of the latter" (p. 20).

Why was the year 2007 so important? At the end of 2006, Facebook finally opened to anyone over thirteen with a valid email, and the social network scaled globally over the course of the following year. Apple released the first iPhone in 2007, combining the world's best media player, a phone, and access to the Internet in one device. The microblogging company Twitter launched in 2007, and Amazon released the first Kindle ebook reader. Google bought YouTube in 2007. Airbnb was conceived that year. The list goes on and on.

Our students will graduate into this changing world of innovation and technology, and we need to do our very best to prepare them for this age of acceleration. As a school leader, you need to take charge of implementing that plan to bring innovation to your school—not just technological innovation, but an innovative approach to teaching and learning.

Eight Administrators Walk Into a Classroom . . .

Eight visiting administrators walk into a classroom. It sounds like the start of a joke, but in fact, it was the genesis of the *NOW Classrooms* series. Here is what we saw there.

It was a second-grade classroom, and groups of students were huddled around a device, actively engaged in creating a script for a video project on mammals and their habitats. Some group members were checking facts collected from various online and print resources, while others were sequencing the script or choosing digital images. Students worked in pairs, trios, and solo, but their interest and engagement in the project was obvious in every configuration. Not one student stopped learning to look at the eight visiting administrators, but when asked, each could explain the purpose of the project in his or her own words. The teacher monitored student progress, supported group problem solving, and reminded students that the project was to be published on the classroom web page in two days.

Across the hall, a third-grade class prepared for its Mystery Skype to start. Mystery Skype (https://education.microsoft.com/skype-in-the-classroom/mystery-skype) is a Microsoft Education initiative: a classroom sets up a Skype session with another classroom, and the students in each class must ask careful yes-or-no questions to determine where in the United States the other class is located. Sitting in teams, the third graders in our building took a few minutes to share strategies for locating the other class, making careful choices about what questions to ask and systematically planning the order in which to ask the questions. Each team's table contained a printed map of the United States and a Chromebook showing Google Maps. Once the session started, the teams eliminated states from the map based on the other class's answers, and they began to zero in on a location. The students were excited to see their questioning strategies in action and talked excitedly about how best to refine them.

In the building's learning center, groups of first graders prepared to film their group book trailers. Every group was independently working on all different types of projects using a variety of tools: apps, laptops, an interactive whiteboard, large paper, digital cameras, books, and a green screen. Every student from each group could explain the learning goals of the activity, as well as the process his or her group had gone through in planning for their trailers.

We all wondered, "Is this kind of engagement normal?" The principal confirmed that it was; students learned like this every day in his school. It was common for him to walk into a classroom and see highly engaged students collaborating on challenging projects and lessons that were aligned to specific learner outcomes. Technology often supported this learning work, and teachers purposefully designed lessons to focus on communicating and critical thinking. The classrooms were rarely quiet.

The Series

Afterward, as we excitedly talked about our school visit, we tried to figure out how best to capture this magic and spread it to other classrooms. Our hope was to help leaders everywhere create schools where active, collaborative, and engaged learning happens for all students, all the time. As a result, we outlined this leadership book that afternoon, along with the four grade-band books of lessons in the *NOW Classrooms* series.

This is the first series we know of that details technology-driven teaching and learning from kindergarten through high school, as well as from the point of view of administrators and building leaders. We intended it to be a potential framework for any school district interested in bringing systemic change to classrooms at all grade levels. What an adventure it has been to write it, and we hope you find this book and the others in the *NOW Classrooms* series useful!

Introduction: The Future Is Ready Now

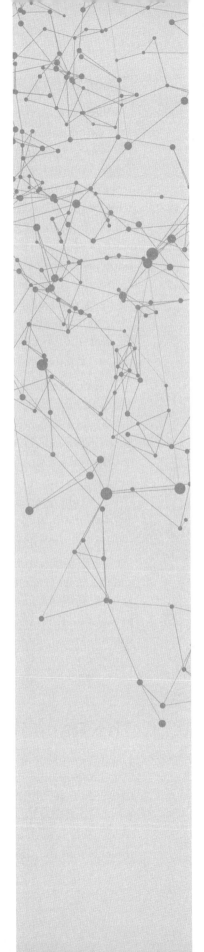

When you walk into a magical classroom, such as the ones we described in the preface to this book, you see change in action. Students lead most of the conversations, and all decisions start with the specific short-term goals that the students formulate. The teacher uses formative assessment data to support students, helping them to make connections as they collaborate on a variety of tasks to meet their goals.

Are there digital tools in the classroom to support the students? Yes, but there are also paper and pencils, books, and much more. In other words, the focus is not on the tools, but on the student-driven learning. All students are laser focused on their personal learning goals as they work on rich, real-world problems that are important to them.

You can feel the energy in these magical classrooms, which we call *NOW classrooms*. We selected that term because our students deserve to thrive in rich, learner-centered classrooms *now*, not in a few months or years. We believe schools are ready to create this type of NOW classroom, typified by technology-supported teaching and learning, and the evidence we've seen bears this belief out. Our goal with this book and this series is to help you create it.

Teaching Before Technology

When computers first became available in schools, students in K–8 could typically only use technology once a week during scheduled computer lab time due to a lack of hardware, infrastructure, and wireless access. Although home environments changed dramatically in the years that followed, few school systems had the finances necessary to replicate the technology-rich environments that students were quickly becoming accustomed to at home. Therefore, access to technology via scheduled weekly computer labs remained the norm for some time, and students' experiences in school could not come close to equaling the innovative creative projects they often engaged in outside with immediate access to a wide variety of devices. In fact, Bill Daggett, president of the International Center for Leadership in Education, often explains this clash of cultures by saying that students leave their homes, where technology is integrated into their daily lives, and then enter the museums we call schools. Similarly, Gayle Gregory and Martha Kaufeldt (2015) claim that most of what adept digital natives commonly have access to at home is prohibited in school.

Outside of school, students have ownership of their learning; whenever a question occurs to them, they can research the answer using technology, or they can imagine and use digital tools to create whatever inspires them at the moment. Such authentic, integrated experiences engage students in learning. As Patti Drapeau (2014) states, "Students are motivated when they feel there is meaning behind what they are doing, which results in taking action" (p. 63). Engagement is inevitable, according to Gregory and Kaufeldt (2015), whenever students communicate, research, analyze, and problem solve real-world, authentic tasks. And as Bob Sullo (2007) tells us, "When teachers and kids are having fun, learning is deeper and stronger, and students maintain the keen desire to learn" (p. 9).

Yet this sustained engagement is in sharp contrast to the way that many administrators and educators structure schools and classrooms. In many schools, this model is changing as devices become more available, but the change has not been an easy one for teachers to adjust to. However, transforming teaching and learning is essential to start preparing students for the demands of today's workplace. Therefore, our team hopes to inspire classrooms, schools, and districts to shift their focus to promoting sustained engagement and collaboration among students.

The Race to the Device

Our broad, shared vision starts with a shared frustration. Over the years, our entire team has experienced many different forms of what we call *the race to the device*. There have been many different devices of the year: tablets, Chromebooks, interactive whiteboards, specialized software, subscription services, and other innovations. In many districts, there is such a focus on acquiring and delivering these miraculous devices to students that they leave many other technology-rollout details to chance. Yet as our co-author Steve says, actually purchasing devices is the easiest part of the process. The big picture of teaching and learning involves a far greater number of factors than the choice of hardware and software platform.

This book is not about educational technology as an end in and of itself; it's about transforming the entire culture of teaching and learning, and technology forms only one part of that overall change. One of the key purposes of this book, then, is to help school leaders completely shift the conversation about technology adoption, moving it out of the technology department and instead working to include all of the school district leaders in a collective vision of change.

As we walk around the building as school leaders, we hope to see groups of students collaborating and creating using technology. What we don't want to see is students or teachers using technology for low-level tasks that aren't directly tied to instruction. For example, we don't want to stop and talk with a group of students about what they are learning, only to have them answer us with the name of an app and nothing more. What we do want to see is students using technology in varied ways to meet learning targets, collaborating with one another, and connecting with students and professionals outside of the school walls. When asked what they are learning, students should tell us about content or skills, not tools. A school must start by devising a vision for teaching and learning. Once that vision is in place, it's time to look at ways to incorporate technology appropriately, using digital tools, apps, or websites to enhance the essential lesson. We cover this visioning and implementation process throughout this book.

This Series

This book, intended for school leaders, is one book in a five-part series. Practicing educators in the Chicago area wrote the other four books. One of our authors, Meg Ormiston, had already written several books before she approached the rest of our collaborative team of twenty-six coauthors about writing this series.

Early in the process, we decided that the project would comprise five books: this one, which is primarily directed at school leaders, and the other four, which are practical, grade-band books for grades K–2, 3–5, 6–8, and 9–12 teachers. Although the content in each grade-band book is different, they are all structured in the same way.

Many schools have added technology into classrooms without seeing student engagement increase. To avoid this issue, we decided to focus heavily on lessons that teachers could begin to use immediately to transform the learning in their classrooms, without necessarily requiring a technology upgrade. We know from our work in schools that teachers and students are at a variety of skill and comfort levels using technology, so we designed our books to meet people where they are and help them develop new skills, ensuring that the focus remains on the quality of the teaching and learning.

Each of the lessons includes age-appropriate technology tools organized using the NOW framework.

- *N* stands for *novice*
- *O* stands for *operational*
- *W* stands for *wow*

Teachers can select lessons in various sections depending on the learning objective they want to achieve and their students' sophistication level with the technology tools involved. For example, in *NOW Classrooms, Grades K–2*, there is a photography lesson titled Snapping and Sharing Photos. It includes the following NOW lesson structure.

- **Novice:** Taking Pictures With a Camera App
- **Operational:** Sequencing Pictures
- **Wow:** Demonstrating Learning Using Pictures

Teachers may, of course, modify the sequence of these lessons to better meet their specific instructional goals. In addition to the lessons, the books provide content connections to all subject areas, including special subjects such as art, music, and physical education. The books also contain classroom management tips, ideas for communicating with parents, teaching tips, and advice on technology use.

Each chapter in the grade-band books ends with a series of discussion questions. The books are not research heavy. The lessons and discussion questions are based on our personal experiences in schools and classrooms. We believe that the discussion questions are valuable for ongoing personal professional development, as well as helpful for clarifying innovation plans. Professional development teams might also use these questions during late-start mornings, early-release days, or other time blocks devoted to on-the-job embedded professional development. They can be useful for personal learning networks as well.

Unlike the grade-band books, this book is specifically structured to help school leaders create and sustain systemic change.

This Book

We have seen the good, the bad, and the ugly in the process of incorporating technology in schools, and, in this book, we've tried to share our practical, honest experiences with the change process and offer real stories drawn from our journeys. Each of the educators involved with this project started with different challenges: demographics, technology, teachers, curriculum, culture, communities, or administrators. That diversity of experience helped this book avoid becoming merely the story of one district and its specific challenges.

We designed this book so that each district and school could customize its basic framework to meet its specific needs. The process we describe—the *why,* the *what,* the *how,* and the *then what,* followed by any necessary rethinking or revision of any of the pieces—may not happen at the same pace, scale, or sequence in all districts. Changing any educational system is complicated. Our hope is that you will find success in helping your team look beyond the technology tools and stay focused on answering teaching and learning questions by deploying the following framework on which we structured this book.

- Why?
  - Seeking support
  - Establishing the visioning process
- What?
  - Communicating the plan
  - Creating teacher activators
- How?
  - Defining and deploying personnel resources
  - Defining and deploying technology resources
  - Defining and deploying financial resources
- Then what?
  - Implementing professional development
  - Connecting the community and showcasing student projects

In this book, chapter 1 starts with the vision itself, or the *why,* which is the most important part of the entire process. The important parts of the framework include the process of seeking support from key stakeholders who will support your innovation throughout its implementation, and the visioning process itself. This chapter also discusses the idea of a growth mindset, which is critical to any innovation's success, as well as the SAMR model (Puentedura, n.d.) for designing and assessing learning opportunities. SAMR, which stands for *substitution, augmentation, modification,* and *redefinition,* is a reflective model intended to help educators integrate technology in purposeful ways.

The planning continues in chapter 2 with the *what.* The key parts of this stage involve communicating the plan to staff, stakeholders, and all other involved parties, as well as creating a small teacher-activator group to begin implementation. This is where the vision from chapter 1 begins to flesh out and the innovation starts to take some serious shape. This chapter also introduces the idea of *getting it out the door.*

Chapter 3 investigates the *how*. This involves defining the essential resources for the implementation of your plan—personnel resources, technology resources, financial resources—and deploying each to good effect.

Chapter 4 discusses the *then what*, a topic that our team believes is a too-often neglected aspect of any successful innovation. This is the plan for encouraging ongoing learning and professional development, as well as for sharing student work, outside of building or district walls, with the community.

Chapter 5 discusses the importance of shifting the vision by revising and updating your innovation over the long term to take best advantage of technological advancement, as well as using data and formative assessment techniques to measure its impact on your building or district.

Finally, we include two appendices. Appendix A provides a full listing of the lesson plans offered in the other four *NOW Classrooms* series books, giving administrators an easy reference for individual grade bands. In appendix B, we've included a list of hundreds of resources, including apps, technology tools, and websites, as well as potentially unfamiliar technology terms. For each listing, we've provided a short description, web link, or other information that teachers and education leaders might find useful in deciding how to incorporate these resources into a classroom.

Similar to the grade-band books, we have included discussion questions at the end of each chapter that can be used for personal reflection or collaborative work with colleagues.

Conclusion

After talking with educators from a variety of schools that have successfully cultivated what we've termed a NOW classroom, we learned that there is no single right way to achieve that result. Every school and district is at a different starting point, and all of them face different challenges. Because of this fact, we wrote this book as a *choose your own adventure*, assuming that leaders would jump to the chapters that best apply to their situations. Your building- or district-level administrative team may also select chapters that specifically address its concerns about technology readiness or effective instructional coaching, as the case may be.

Whatever path you choose to start with, we hope it leads to creating a school full of classrooms where student learning is active, engaging, and purposeful. We suspected we were on the right track with our approach when one peer reviewer told us, "This book should be given to every teacher in a 1:1 classroom." We believe you will agree.

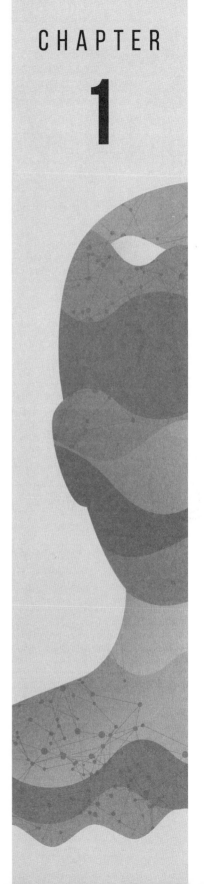

The *Why*: Creating and Communicating a Vision for Change

When contemplating any instructional innovation, the most important question a school district can ask itself is, "Why are we doing this?" That *why*—an inspiring and instructional vision for innovation—needs to be at the very heart of a district's purpose. Yet all districts wrestle not only with the best way to articulate that vision but also with the best way to communicate it to the stakeholders who will support its implementation. This chapter discusses the importance of stakeholder support and offers advice on beginning the visioning process. We begin by addressing the challenge of helping everyone in a school building adopt the growth mindset necessary for successful innovation.

Establishing Growth Mindsets

The process of building NOW classrooms begins with changing your school community's underlying culture. As a building or district leader, you can't simply decree that the culture must change; you need a cyclical plan that cultivates it. The plan involves:

- Creating a vision for changing classroom culture and incorporating technology

- Implementing experiments to build that vision

- Assessing the success or failure of your experiments
- Revising the initial vision accordingly

In other words, successful innovation requires you to follow a cycle of continuous improvement through ongoing testing and reflection.

This type of rapid acceleration requires a whole new approach on the part of everyone involved. Incorporating new technology in the classroom requires flexibility and adaptability. Carol Dweck (2008), a renowned Stanford professor, coined the term *growth mindset*. By Dweck's definition, a person with a growth mindset believes he or she has the ability to grow, learn, and change. By contrast, a person with a fixed mindset believes he or she doesn't have the ability to effect change. As educators, we must use a growth mindset in both our language and our actions to move forward in our improvement of learning for ourselves and our students.

Our goal in every school should be to encourage growth mindsets in everyone in order to prepare our students for an ever-changing world in which they can thrive. To that end, we believe every teacher, parent, coach, and school leader will benefit from reading Dweck's (2008) book, *Mindset: The New Psychology of Success*. We believe that to achieve lasting change with staff and students, everyone—not only students but also stakeholders —must develop a growth mindset in order to approach the process of teaching and learning with digital tools.

Many readers, after finishing the preceding paragraph, will already be able to hear the grumbling from their staff. A fixed mindset does not marry well with the technology innovation we write about; without the belief that it's possible to become facile with technology through practice, stakeholders will throw in the towel and quit after hitting the first bump in the road. But we suspect that with the increasing prevalence of technology in daily life, the grumbling might not be as bad as it was back in 2007, when many teachers were still struggling to adjust to email and file management.

We all understand that change is hard, period. We also know that it's our responsibility in education to prepare students for the real world. In other words, it's our job to prepare our students to embrace change, and that means we need to understand how to embrace it ourselves.

To prepare for an effective vision for change, school leaders need to start by building a growth mindset with all the adults in the school, from the front office to the bus drivers. The language everyone uses with other adults and students should be focused on growth mindset. Used daily, growth mindset language will help to expedite a successful technology innovation. Look for opportunities to acknowledge flexibility and adaptability versus rigidity and a desire to maintain the status quo.

One effective way to get started with this is to have the building staff read Dweck's (2008) *Mindset* as a group. The book has a companion website, Mindset Works (www.mindsetworks.com), which staff can use to supplement this reading group. *The Growth Mindset Coach: A Teacher's Month-by-Month Handbook for Empowering Students to Achieve* by Annie Brock and Heather Hundley (2016) is also helpful for bringing a growth mindset into the classroom itself. As you read the book together as a staff, encourage everyone to consider the ways in which a growth mindset might operate in their personal lives and with their families, not just in their jobs as educators.

It may be helpful to read this book as a staff over the summer, since during the school year it can be more difficult to initiate work around a growth mindset while also doing everything else that goes into leading a school. However, if you lay the groundwork for a growth mindset over the summer, you can continue to build on it regularly during the year. For example, you might start every learning event with one key example of growth mindset that you have seen staff or students exhibit. If you lead in this way, soon everyone will start to notice and share his or her own experiences with growth mindset, and the concept will become part of the culture.

One way to start cultivating a growth mindset in the building is to create an empty bulletin board with the word *yet* by itself in the middle and ask each of your teachers to set a goal for the year, with each goal focused around the idea of *yet*. For example, a teacher who wants to work on increasing her students' facility with online research might define her goal as *My students don't know how to do good research online . . . yet.* The staff then writes those goals on colored cards and posts them to the bulletin board, encouraging a very public focus on growth mindset.

Teachers can also start to introduce growth mindsets to students by asking them to create their own *yet* bulletin board to define their goals for the year. Soon, all staff and students will have embraced the idea that anything is possible with a growth mindset.

We know that establishing a culture of growth mindsets will not happen overnight—change takes practice, as a growth mindset itself states! But it is the right thing for the school's culture, and the success of any innovation ultimately depends on it.

Supporting Stakeholders

To develop a complete and satisfying innovation—and to ensure that there are no roadblocks to successfully implementing it—districts should ensure that all key stakeholders have a voice when beginning to dream up any major initiative. One of the first steps to take when attempting to answer the question *why* is to identify those key stakeholders and to engage them in the visioning process.

Depending on the individual district, the key stakeholders who need to be involved may include school board members, administrators (including technology directors and business officials), teachers, students, parents, or community members. Some districts may already have district leadership teams, which typically include representatives from all of these stakeholder groups. If your district doesn't—or if it does, but doesn't include some of the key groups we've mentioned—be sure to invite representatives from outside to ensure a minimum of misunderstanding (or interference) later in the process.

In particular, it's important to involve school board members from the beginning and to ensure that they're clear about the *why* behind your vision. Imagine what might happen if several districts in your area purchased devices and subsequently received a lot of publicity. Members of your own board might be concerned that perhaps the district is more interested in trying to "keep up with the Joneses" by hopping on the new device bandwagon than it is with improving instruction or engaging in a learning innovation. To prevent these concerns from cropping up in your own district, and to avoid any critical miscommunications, it's very important to involve board members from the outset. Remember: school board members are the stakeholders who represent the community by voting for or against any funding initiatives for infrastructure, devices, or other learning supports. That means that they're the ones to whom parents and other community residents will address questions about how their money is being spent.

It's also imperative for the district's business officials to be involved in planning and forecasting from the beginning, as the vision may require additional implementation funds for professional development, staffing, or other infrastructure. If business officials are involved early in the process, they'll be more likely to understand the why behind your innovation, which means that they can argue persuasively on its behalf when it comes to budgeting. This is very important in today's economic climate, where there are many competing priorities for dwindling public resources.

Most important, however, as we'll stress throughout the remainder of this book: it's imperative to continue dialogue and communication well beyond these initial consultations regarding the *why* of your innovation. Without information or updates on the progress of implementing your vision, the support you corral early on can quickly drop off.

Developing a Vision

Now that you have the right stakeholders identified, it's time to begin working with them to develop a vision. Here are some of the questions we've used in the past to guide our thinking.

- What do we want our schools to look like in the future, and how can we plan for that today?

- What does quality teaching and learning look like with technology?

- Why is it critical for our students to connect with one another beyond the walls of the classroom?

- What skills do our students need in order to be successful in the future world outside of schools?

Note that none of these questions necessarily depends on any specific devices, platforms, or other resources. At this early stage of the innovation process, we have found that it's imperative to keep the focus on teaching and learning rather than on devices, infrastructure, and technology personnel. The nuts and bolts will come later to fill out the details of the vision. For now, the desired student outcomes are more important than any specific implementation plans. To that end, in this section, we write about some big-picture items to keep in the forefront of your thinking as you contemplate the *why* of your vision, including a cautionary note regarding potential counterproductive decision making, a look at essential 21st century skills—the four Cs (Partnership for 21st Century Learning, 2015) and the SAMR model—and how to manage the visioning process.

The Paper Police: A Cautionary Note

Real systemic change requires big thinking and a lot of focused energy. But most important, it requires a good, forward-thinking answer to the question of *why*—one that always centers around the idea of student learning.

We caution you to consider what might happen when the will for systemic technology change isn't accompanied by a strong vision for transforming learning with all key stakeholders and staff members on board. Consider the following possible scenario: a district administrator representing the business office visits an elementary school to speak at a faculty meeting. During the meeting, the administrator presents colorful slides showing paper usage in the building and the total monthly overage charges on the copy machines. The cost of the paper and the overage charges are more than what the district would spend on 1:1 Chromebooks for every student.

Clearly, one might conclude that it was time for a change. However, instead of seriously thinking about why the school was using the amount of paper it used—and thus about how the school might rethink its teaching and learning objectives not only in order to use less paper but to be more generally effective—the school chooses to implement a more stringent copying policy. The new policy requires that teachers use individual codes to log in to the copy machine so that the district office can create a leaderboard of copy activity which will then be used to celebrate the staff members with the lowest number of copies each week.

In other words, the administration has become the paper police. This is not only a misuse of the administrators' time but also a regressive vision for change, not a productive one. As more digital devices are in the hands of students, paper-and-pencil tasks need to be modified to harness the power of the technology. Student projects should be part of a new digital workflow where work is submitted through a classroom learning management system (LMS) instead of on paper.

The Four Cs and the SAMR Model

In 2015, Partnership for 21st Century Learning—a coalition of policymakers, education leaders, and business community members—released a research series on the key skills needed for success in the 21st century (Partnership for 21st Century Learning, 2015). The so-called four Cs—*communication, collaboration, critical thinking,* and *creativity*—used to be called the *soft skills* needed for future success. In the 21st century, however, they're more often referred to as the *super skills* of the future.

When you walk through the halls of your school to assess whether the innovations your staff have implemented are working, look for evidence of the four Cs in action. Additionally, any vision your team develops should include the four Cs as well as the expectation that students will master them. In designing your innovation, begin by expecting teachers to be willing to change teaching and learning in their classrooms, and expect them to be responsible for sharing artifacts and projects their students create.

How should teaching and learning change? One effective model for describing good learning is the SAMR model, a framework for describing the ways that students might use technology in the service of learning. Ruben Puentedura (n.d.), founder and president of the information consulting firm Hippasus (www.hippasus.com), developed the SAMR model. He designed it to classify instructional opportunities that advancing technology makes possible. This model, which many districts and states have adopted, gives schools and districts a shared language to use when restructuring lessons to incorporate technology. All the authors of this series framed professional development around the SAMR model before, during, and after their technology rollout and found it useful to refer to while developing the *why* of the innovation.

The SAMR model breaks down into four distinct categories.

1. **Substitution** involves using a digital tool to perform a traditional task. For example, students might use a word processing program to type a paper they otherwise would have written by hand.

2. **Augmentation** involves using a digital tool to achieve a significant functional improvement on the traditional tool. For example, a student might type a paper in a Google Doc, which he or she can then share directly with the teacher for immediate feedback.

3. **Modification** involves significant changes to a task's nature and purpose. For example, students might use Padlet not only to share with the teacher but to collaborate and comment to one another in ways that would have been impossible for a traditional word processor.

4. **Redefinition** involves the students performing tasks that would have been altogether inconceivable without the digital tool. For example, students might collaborate on a paper while at separate locations on a class trip, or they might create a multiauthored website that discusses various aspects of a topic and invites others to engage with the site.

Although simple, the SAMR model can help all staff members start to understand and reflect on specific innovation goals. For example, when Meg visited Maercker School District 60 in 2014, iPads provided for student use were filled with designated apps. However, most of those were low-level, skill-practice apps, with no way for the teacher to monitor student progress. When the district planning team introduced the SAMR model and teachers began to internalize it, the team realized that this was a missed opportunity. Students had substituted the digital tool for the traditional tools, but tasks were still the same; in other words, the *quality* of learning hadn't changed. Therefore, the planning team decided to clean off a majority of the practice apps, replacing them with content-creation apps. Soon students were screencasting, making movies, designing presentations, and sharing them everywhere. These were tasks that would have been impossible with previous technology, and this was the kind of learning that a technology innovation should bring about.

One important note: at the modification and redefinition levels, the students, rather than the teacher, often direct the learning. Because these levels are where student ownership is the most prevalent and most powerful, those familiar with the SAMR model often refer to modification and redefinition tasks as *above the line*. Despite this term, the SAMR model does not describe a hierarchal ladder of tasks arranged from worst to best. The student learning outcome is the most important thing, and not all outcomes are most appropriately achieved through redefinition tasks. Yet it is still important to try to incorporate different model levels into the overall vision for your innovation. By doing so, you can help to avoid the possibility of classrooms remaining stagnant. Figure 1.1 (page 14) offers a succinct depiction of the SAMR model, with additional examples.

The Process Itself

To increase the likelihood of developing a successful vision, a school can group the stakeholders and educators involved in the visioning process into teams designed to blend diverse viewpoints. For example, teams might be composed of members from different schools, or they might involve different job roles within the same school. By listening to varied opinions, team members can more easily create a vision that includes all stakeholders' ideas.

Three key aspects of the vision are that it must be aligned with the district's overall vision (if, indeed, that is something different), written succinctly so it can be remembered easily and reflected on frequently, and focused on learning rather than devices. When it is finalized, the vision needs to be memorialized in writing. This could be in a variety of formats, such as a statement or bulleted list, with all members of the group signing off on the document.

For example, a vision might be, "Preparing today's learners to excel in tomorrow's world." This mantra could serve as both the overall vision and the innovation's vision. Because learners are the subject, it encompasses all stakeholders: students, staff, and parents. *Tomorrow's world* implies a sense of urgency in that the vision is not for some

Transformation

Redefinition: Technology allows for the creation of new tasks, previously inconceivable. For example, create a narrated Google Earth guided tour and share this online.

Modification: Technology allows for significant task redesign. For example, use Google Earth layers, such as Panoramio and 360 Cities, to research locations.

Enhancement

Augmentation: Technology acts as direct tool substitute, with functional improvement. For example, use Google Earth rulers to measure the distance between two places.

Substitution: Technology acts as a direct tool substitute, with no functional change. For example, use Google Earth instead of an atlas to locate a place.

Source: Adapted from Puentedura, n.d.

Figure 1.1: The SAMR model.

distant future, but it also encompasses the greater concept of *tomorrow* and all the changes and adaptations that may be needed as learning research and technological advancements continually improve.

This overall visioning process might take a few hours or a few days, depending on where the school or district is starting from, the resources available, or the views of the stakeholders around the table. At the end of this process, however, it's imperative to make sure that the vision is carefully articulated and recorded, and most important, that the group agrees on it. You will need to communicate this vision to classroom leaders or other stakeholders who were unable to take part in the visioning process, and this process will go much more smoothly if you begin by carefully articulating and recording your intentions.

Conclusion

As David Jakes (2016), a consultant in educational technology and design thinking, writes on his blog:

Of course the real game of improving education is about changing the educational mindset of schools and how schools serve learning. That's the responsibility of everyone in the organization and means focusing on the essence of what is important in the context of the growth and development of children.

And that's an incredibly complex and difficult thing to do.

It requires much more than playing with LittleBits, breaking out of a box, creating online worksheets in Google Docs, or being a genius on Friday afternoon. It requires teaching like a human being rather than like a pirate. It requires more than several teachers in classrooms doing interesting things in isolation. It requires sustained focus and effort and not being distracted or misled by the latest Twitter flavor of the month or the trendy keynoter shouting from the highest stage about the newest thing.

Our team agrees with David; in our experience, this work is complex and incredibly difficult. But we firmly believe that this hard work is exactly what every student deserves. Therefore, when developing our vision and listening to stakeholder needs, we always need to stay grounded in the understanding that the challenges ahead are intended for our students. We do this work for their future, not for our past.

DISCUSSION QUESTIONS

Consider the following questions for personal reflection or in collaborative work with colleagues.

▸ Why are you considering a learning innovation using technology?

▸ How does your school already employ a growth mindset? In what ways might you cultivate this to a greater degree?

▸ Who needs to be on the stakeholder team, and why?

▸ Why is it critical to communicate your vision and plan?

▸ What are three questions you will include in your visioning process?

▸ What examples of the four Cs have you seen in your building? How much do you build on them?

▸ How would you describe the SAMR model to a group? Why is this model helpful?

▸ What role do you see your business office playing in this process?

▸ In his blog post, Jakes (2016) describes the need for sustained focus and effort. What points in this chapter support his claim?

▸ What is one specific thing from this chapter that you will share with a colleague?

The *What*: Planning the Launch

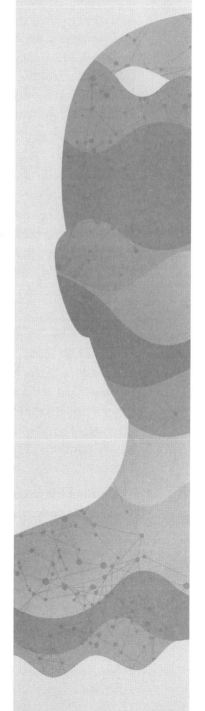

Now that the vision for innovation is in place and key stakeholders are on board, it's time to move forward with the *what*—in other words, the actual plans for implementation. Using information about stakeholder needs gleaned through the visioning process, you can begin to develop a specific implementation plan based on your district or building's starting point while keeping the end goal in mind. In this chapter, we explain the importance of communicating the plan to all stakeholders, as well as the importance of using a teacher-activator team to drive pilot programs.

Communicating the Plan

From the outset, there should be frequent communication with all stakeholders about the vision for innovation on which you and your planning team have agreed. People tend to fear what they do not understand, and the time you invest in planning your strategy for communication will pay big dividends moving forward. Stakeholders will be more likely to understand the purpose and goals behind the plan—in particular how it will benefit student learning and growth. Additionally, gathering feedback about the plan can uncover myriad questions, which can help ensure they are addressed.

This is especially true when it comes to communicating your vision to those inside the building or district. When information spreads to those outside your immediate staff, the people inside will be the ones expected to clear up any misunderstandings about exactly what your vision involves. If you don't provide stakeholders with good information about your intentions, they will create their own ideas, which aren't likely to be accurate or helpful. For example, if districts allow students to take devices home, a parent may observe her child engaging in games (not assigned by the teacher) and falsely assume that these are representative of what devices are primarily used for during instruction. This could cause a skeptic to surmise that kids just play games all day. Teachers are often the front line of communication with parents, and they need to understand how to effectively address unfounded claims and misunderstandings. This means effectively communicating, keeping everyone on the same page, and getting the plan out the door.

Don't Be Afraid to Overcommunicate

There are many ways to communicate with stakeholders about your *why*, and we encourage you to use all of them. For some stakeholders, a real-time visit to the classroom can help them witness transformational learning in action. If you keep the doors open, skeptics will be able to see your intended goals for themselves, rather than relying on your meaning that may get lost in the translation to newsletters, tweets, or other forms of getting out information. Parent information sessions can be designed where students present to parents in order to share how lessons integrated technology into their academic learning. Even kindergarten students will be eager to share their innovative projects with parents, making student ambassadors ideal advocates for your innovation and its focus on higher learning levels.

Beyond direct encounters with students and teachers, you can and should make use of all available media. This might include using traditional media, such as newsletters or other mailings from the building or district, or potentially reaching out to local newspapers interested in the details of a new major technology initiative. Digital venues, such as social media or municipal or district websites, can also act as powerful tools for getting the message out. Twitter and Facebook pages in particular are among the ultimate technology platforms to vividly communicate learning in action; a picture of your students in action is always worth a thousand words.

Whatever the medium, clear communication is essential in helping all stakeholders understand the *why* behind an instructional innovation, although the form of your message may differ depending on the audience. When communicating internally, for example, you might use vocabulary that's common among educators to clarify examples and to provide a more detailed description of the overall vision. External communication, however, requires that you present the vision using broader ideas and generally more accessible terminology.

In all cases, it's advantageous to carefully map out your plans for communicating your vision over the short and long term. Decide on the media you intend to use, the level of terminology and specificity appropriate to each channel, and the specific ways that you intend to make classrooms, pilot programs, or student work available via classroom visits or social media posts. Once the journey begins, there will most likely be multiple distractions involved with the *what* and *how* of implementation, so it will pay off to define a clear strategy from the outset for communicating the *why*.

Get Everyone on the Same Page, Literally

As of the writing of this book, we've found that most schools we have worked with have migrated to G Suite for Education for managing collaborative documents and cloud storage. Although there are similar platforms (such as Microsoft Education and Apple Education), we advocate for this platform as a key tool in the success of your implementation. In particular, Google Docs—free, collaborative documents that every teacher or staff member in the building can log in to and work on simultaneously—can allow instantaneous and responsive communication and feedback among the various people responsible for specifically implementing your vision. (If G Suite for Education features, such as Google Drive, are new to you as a school leader, ask your staff to help you find someone who can teach you how to use them.)

One tactic we've found useful is keeping everyone on the same page—literally—by using a single, cloud-based shared document for every faculty meeting throughout the year. Figure 2.1 shows a template that can be recreated as a Google Doc and used for this purpose. This one document should contain all the notes, questions, comments, and action steps created at each faculty meeting. You could restrict this exclusively to matters related to your technology vision, but in our experience, having multiple documents for a single school year is inefficient and creates a technology distraction instead of helping to organize the group.

Date	Topic	Details	Follow-Up

Figure 2.1: Shared document template for meetings.

*Visit **go.SolutionTree.com/technology** for a free reproducible version of this figure.*

Using one shared document also streamlines communication. (Just imagine how much email you could skip once it's in place!) Team leaders can automatically create the year-long meeting notes and minutes in the document in real time during the meeting itself, and you will be able to look in on what individual grade-level teams are discussing and become aware of any important action items. The system pays dividends in the future, as well; for example, new team members can use last year's notes to get up to speed with ongoing discussions within the staff.

Encourage your staff to add their comments, questions, and personal notes about any of the action items. Don't worry about losing anything. Documents shared on cloud-storage platforms like Google Drive or Microsoft OneDrive automatically save changes as you go. Every document also includes a revision history, which means that if someone deletes an important section, the group can easily retrieve what was lost.

Your staff may struggle with the adjustment to coordinating communication via shared documents, but in our experience, participants quickly adjust. One suggestion is to prepare for the school year by practicing with a collaborative summer reading of Dweck's (2008) *Mindset* (as we suggested in chapter 1). Everyone's notes on the book can be organized in a three-column chart, as shown in figure 2.2. Each staff member records the page number in the first column, notes about the book in the middle column, and reflections about connections between the book and their individual experiences in the third column.

Page Number	Notes	Reflections and Connections

Figure 2.2: Collaborative reading template.

*Visit **go.SolutionTree.com/technology** for a free reproducible version of this figure.*

This not only allows your entire staff to be active collaborators while studying growth mindsets but also helps them become comfortable with using shared documents for buildingwide or districtwide communication during the actual school year.

Get It Out the Door

Change is never easy, particularly in the education world where practices haven't evolved all that much in the last hundred years. For example, when Meg began to work on instructional technology integration with Maercker School District 60 in 2014, she introduced the concept of sharing student work from pilot programs via social media, and the district's school leaders were apprehensive. Student interaction with a global audience was not common practice.

But everything changed when the school leaders actually viewed the short snippets of student learning that the district's pilot teachers had posted to Twitter. These snippets provided daily examples of the practical changes to classroom instruction occurring during the innovation, as well as clarity about the *why* of the innovation. In particular, the leaders noticed that as soon as the learners discovered that there was an authentic audience for their work, they showed an increased level of engagement in their learning. Gregory and Kaufeldt (2015) concur:

> Students don't get the same thrill of handing in a project to a teacher as they do from demonstrating their originality on the internet to friends, family, and strangers. They get feedback from everywhere. We need to let go of some control and let students create and build success for their futures in the global marketplace. (p. 143)

By using social media to get the message out the door, the district could communicate to stakeholders that the students were using the four Cs (Partnership for 21st Century Learning, 2015) in their learning. This sent a strong message to our communities about the value of the project, which removed some concerns about implementation. Do not underestimate the power of social media on your journey; it is truly invaluable!

Creating Teacher Activators

Rather than the term *pilot teachers*, we use the term *teacher activators*, a term Michael Fullan coined to refer to the fact that these teachers activate students' learning in the classroom (Fullan & Donnelly, 2013). The label is unimportant; call your teachers whatever you want, as long as you establish an effective pilot group, understand what a sound pilot program looks like, and prepare for what steps to take after the pilot.

Pilot Groups

Many of our districts used a pilot approach to build capacity for the learning innovation by creating teacher activators and providing targeted professional development for those participants. Communication from a pilot implementation can be a great way to keep internal stakeholders informed about the implementation's progress. Allowing a small group to test the waters also helps to detect potential challenges to avoid during a larger-scale rollout.

In general, the following steps will help leaders develop an effective pilot program.

- The administrators should identify key teachers as teacher activators.
- Teachers should identify students as student activators.
- The visioning team should develop a comprehensive plan for measuring and reporting on the results of the program to the entire building or district.

When determining candidates for teacher activators, two things are important. First, choose teachers who are willing to take risks and *really* test the effectiveness of the program. These teachers should be prepared to implement with fidelity while also taking risks. They should have a strong grasp of the curriculum and a vision for where technology can be integrated. Second, be sure that the teachers you choose understand that it's safe to share their successes—as well as the challenges they encounter—with you and other administrators. As participants share failures, it should be done in a setting where they are not judged personally or professionally. Structures should be established to encourage teachers to share what has worked well, what didn't work, and hypotheses as to why. This way, you'll have accurate data about the pilot program's effects, making it far more likely that the full-scale rollout succeeds.

A Sample Pilot Program

When Meg began working with Maercker School District 60 in 2014, she taught a professional development class as part of the district's internal university. The district used this internal university to support a pilot focused on learning innovation with technology integration. At the time of the pilot, the district's access to technology devices was extremely limited. The K–2 and 3–5 buildings had computer labs that students attended once a week for forty-five minutes, while the middle school had laptops on carts that teachers had to check out. Access to devices for any extended period was essentially impossible. The district was considering moving toward a 1:1 initiative, but it first wanted to see how increased access to devices, apps, software, and coaching would change instruction.

We present the details of that district's pilot program in figure 2.3 to give you an example of the broad outlines of a similar program that your own district or school might be able to use.

When the teacher activators reported these experiences and findings to the school board, their enthusiasm and passion radiated throughout the room. Board members stated that they learned a great deal about how technology integration can transform learning and that they had a greater understanding of why it was essential to move toward increased access for students and teachers.

Sample Pilot: Four Cs of Instructional Design (Instructional Technology Pilot)

Course description: This course is for K–8 teachers interested in piloting new approaches and methods to create a 21st century classroom. Space is limited to one teacher per grade level. The application and selection process is outlined as follows.

Facilitators: Building learning and technology integration coaches and middle school library information specialist

Participants are expected to complete the following activities to receive credit.

- Participate in introductory meeting.
- Participate in training and lesson-design planning with facilitators through provided release time.
- Engage in the online Edmodo and Wikispace Professional Learning Network to share experiences and artifacts.
- Design and implement lessons based on the principles of the four Cs and the integration of technology.
- Share experiences with colleagues at School Improvement Plan (SIP) or staff meetings.
- Provide feedback on the effectiveness of the technology devices and software applications used during the pilot.
- Participate in a debrief meeting.
- Participate in a group presentation at the end-of-year board meeting.

Pilot participants will receive:

- Specialized training and support on 21st century instructional design
- Access to tech devices (K–2 iPads; 3–8 laptops) during your choice of English language arts, mathematics, science, or social studies block for five days in April or May

Pilot findings:

- Coaching support and increased access to devices allowed students to collaborate within the classroom and a global community.
- Student access to information and the ability to share their work was timely (students did not have wait a week to return to the computer lab or for the laptop cart to be available).
- Students demonstrated higher engagement levels.
- Reluctant writers and readers demonstrated their knowledge through voice typing and video recordings.
- It was easier to embed student choice into lesson design; students had choice about their topic of study and how to share their knowledge.

Source: © 2017 by Maercker School District 60. Used with permission.

Figure 2.3: Sample pilot project document.

💬 DISCUSSION QUESTIONS

Consider the following questions for personal reflection or in collaborative work with colleagues.

- ▶ What is the best way to communicate with your stakeholders: print, email, on the school website, or some other means?

- ▶ How will you overcome resistance to the idea of communicating your plan's objectives by sharing student work?

- ▶ How will you communicate your plan to the broader community?

- ▶ What instructional framework is in place for lesson redesign?

- ▶ We use the term *teacher activators* for our pilot teachers. What term will you use, and why?

- ▶ What roadblocks to change do you think you might experience when creating teacher activators? Is there anyone you already have in mind within your building or district for this role?

- ▶ What is your opinion about pilot projects for teachers? Why do you think that?

- ▶ Why involve students as ambassadors for your pilot program?

- ▶ What detail from the sample pilot program do you find most relevant to your own school or district's situation?

- ▶ What is one thing from this chapter you plan on sharing with a colleague?

After the Pilot

In Maercker School District 60, conversations and planning were going on between departments for the entire duration of the classroom pilot. The pilot ended with a high level of momentum, and participants were eager to plan for the following school year. Every stakeholder could now articulate the reasons for the initiative and each participant agreed on moving forward with it on a larger scale.

The pilot led to a full-scale implementation effort the following year. Over the summer, staff cleared the computer labs of their desktops and moved the working machines to individual classrooms. This opened new learning spaces for portable devices. This equipment shift also represented a shift in thinking for teachers, who had been used to going to the computer lab for technology instruction each week. The change helped to create the understanding that this learning innovation was designed to prepare students for technology-filled futures where learning might happen anytime and anywhere.

Conclusion

After the first year of full implementation, the capacity for leadership and the number of in-house experts both grew exponentially, with the initial team now well into the double digits. This facilitated even greater differentiation of professional learning opportunities for staff who hadn't yet become involved. A wide variety of staff members led summer learning offerings with participants from all levels of responsibility in the district. Primary, intermediate, and middle school teachers, specialists, support staff, and administrators all learned shoulder-to-shoulder together, growing their knowledge and skills.

This is an absolutely desirable outcome. We can't just hope that active learning happens in the classroom; we need to model it as often as possible for the staff. Change takes practice with learners of all ages. By having a clear sense of the *what* of your vision—a plan for communication throughout and a pilot group to provide a clear, scalable model for implementation—that practice will pay off and will lead to a successful rollout of your vision.

The *How*: Defining and Deploying Essential Resources

Imagine walking into a district as a new administrator and realizing that it has purchased massive amounts of technology with no plan for professional development, no plan for implementation, and ultimately, no plan for technology integration to improve student achievement. This seems like an impossible mistake for a district to make, and yet it happened to an administrator on our writing team. To avoid a looming disaster, and to quickly get the devices into the hands of students, the administrator had to enlist the help of an outside consultant to assess the situation and create a meaningful plan to shift instructional practices in a way that was consistent with the technology the district had already purchased.

This is why the *how* of your vision is important. Ensuring that there's a plan in place for the practical implementation details seems like common sense. Unfortunately, the preceding scenario is all too common in schools. To avoid interrupting normal learning and teaching—as well as to avoid a crisis such as the one our administrator faced—it's important to carefully define these resources before beginning to implement a large-scale innovation. These resources may include new personnel (or new roles for existing personnel), technology upgrades, or financial resources to support the previous two categories in a way that makes budgetary sense.

Now that the visioning process has shown *why* you're acting, and a teacher-activator-driven pilot has shown *what* you need to do, it's time to determine *how* it will happen in specific terms. This phase of the process is where the rubber meets the road, so in this chapter we will outline how you can define and deploy the personnel, technology, and financial resources that are essential to a successful implementation.

Defining and Deploying Personnel Resources

Implementing instructional technology in the classroom usually results in a need to review, adjust, and sometimes create roles for district and school staff. By revising and drafting job titles and descriptions, you can help to clarify what specific staff members are expected to do. Some examples of key roles you need to support building administrators, teachers, and students may include:

- **Director of curriculum**—This is a district-level position, responsible for collaborating with the superintendent, building administrators, teachers, and other key stakeholders to develop the instructional expectations for technology use. Once this group develops these expectations, the director of curriculum coordinates with the director of instructional technology to ensure that they can be effectively met. Additionally, this role coordinates plans for professional development.

- **Director of instructional technology**—This is a district-level position, responsible for partnering with other administrators to understand the educational goals for using technology and for ensuring that the infrastructure meets those goals. You will want to provide multiple opportunities for the director of instructional technology to meet and coordinate with instructional leaders. This role is also responsible for ordering, cataloguing, and coordinating maintenance of all equipment.

- **Technology aide or specialist**—This is a building-level position, charged with device setup and repair and maintaining other equipment. As new applications or subscriptions become available, this staff member ensures that these are properly installed on each device.

- **Instructional coach**—Instructional coaches provide professional learning support to teachers and teams. Their role includes training staff on how to use various applications and software while focusing on standards and learning first. More important, coaches partner with teachers to develop student-centered goals that utilize technology to support instruction or data gathering. If possible, assign one coach to each building.

- **Learning and technology integration coach**—This building- or district-level position focuses on instructional design and higher-level learning skills that integrate technology. Staff in this position may have formerly been called *computer teachers*. In this new role, learning and technology integration coaches train teachers and support learning.

- **Computer lab aide**—This building-level role assumes clerical tasks once led by computer teachers, such as device maintenance as assigned and troubleshooting.

- **School library information specialist**—The school library information specialist, formerly called a *media center director*, should facilitate access to information through a variety of resources, including technology. This building-level position is also responsible for teaching students how to ethically access, interpret, and use information.

Each district will have its own staffing needs, of course. In Maercker School District 60, personnel previously labeled as *computer teachers* advocated for changing their job title to *learning and technology integration coaches*. These staff also rewrote their job descriptions to minimize their traditional tasks (such as practicing keyboarding, introducing software, and troubleshooting computers) and to instead emphasize building 21st century skills within the building (such as improving instructional practices within the classroom and coaching teachers and staff on technology). Computer lab aides then took on the responsibilities of the integration coaches' traditional tasks, freeing certified teachers to work more directly on implementing the innovation.

The director of the school media center in this same district had traditionally and primarily functioned as a librarian. However, some of the traditional library duties had become obsolete; for example, at the middle school level, students had learned to handle checkout through a self-serve kiosk. In response to this shift, the media director shifted some of her own traditional library responsibilities to a dedicated assistant and was thus able to free up time to become an integral part of instructional planning teams, as well as to work more closely with the school's STEM center and maker space. As a result, her title changed to *school library information specialist,* a term that better captured the idea that 21st century students often obtain information outside of actual library resources. Rather than managing library materials, she instead helped teach students how to critically engage with and ethically use the information they accessed.

Remember that whatever roles you establish or change, it's important to review and adjust staffing budgets to ensure that you have funds for all new positions.

Once you have determined your personnel needs, you'll want to take steps to ensure a smooth transition. You can accomplish this by directing support and dealing with detractors.

Directing Support

There will be cheerleaders and enthusiastic early adopters of any innovation, and then there will be those teachers who hope to close their doors and wait for the dust to settle. It is the job of the building administrator to keep all learners involved in the process of shifting the school culture around preparing students for college and career success; however, it's challenging to accomplish this in a time when many traditional staff roles around technology need to change to support new innovation. Consequently, it's critical to ensure that recalcitrant teachers have a firm grasp on where to get support while adjusting to the new way of doing things.

Providing a written guiding document for staff to refer to when they need support will help align tasks and projects to the appropriate staff member. Table 3.1 provides an example of how this information can be clearly outlined. Each district is unique, so the actual content may vary depending on the setting.

Table 3.1: Technology Support Contact List

Issue or Question	Who to Contact
"My printer or device isn't working."	Technology aide
"I would like to have tablets for my students rather than laptops."	Director of instructional technology
"I see that a new application is installed—how do I use it?"	Instructional coach
"I found a great new website to use with my students. How can I get a subscription?"	Principal
"How can I help my students determine whether an online resource contains valid research?"	School library information specialist

Dealing With Detractors

Any learner group includes diverse viewpoints, and the kind of tech-rock-star teacher who's always enthusiastic about innovation is only one part of the equation. Some of the adults in the school district may not be ready for your innovation, and as a result, they may drag their feet on implementing it or attempt to block it outright. Building and district leaders should be prepared to productively deal with those detractors by creating a clear expectation that everyone on staff needs to focus positive energy on the innovation, even if technology is a challenge for him or her. This innovation is not about the comfort of the teachers; it's about building a positive future for students. Help reluctant teachers along the journey by celebrating small steps toward the vision.

Balancing everyone's needs while furthering the goals of the innovation is the real art of leadership. Some practical things may help, however; in order to feel supported, every adult in the building needs clear expectations, timely and specific feedback, and a sense of being reinforced and encouraged on this new focus on learning. Some teachers will need a different level of support than other teachers, and finding that balance daily can be a challenge due to all the other demands of a leader's job. Despite efforts, detractors may still present some resistance. Individual conversations to clarify expectations and job responsibilities can help ensure staff members understand that the integration of technology is not a matter of "if" but "when." It can also be beneficial to include technology integration as a part of the staff evaluation process. This can help clarify expectations, in writing, and provide robust opportunities for feedback. In the case of individuals not being able to integrate technology, even with extensive support, a remediation plan may be needed.

Defining and Deploying Technology Resources

Most technology innovations require a digital platform that students and teachers can use on their devices. By *digital platform* we are referring specifically to software. Each provider has its own requirements for registration and setup. If your district hasn't decided on a platform, it is important to do so as early as possible in order to review and evaluate the available options and determine the one that's the most appropriate for your overall plan. The district technology director also needs time to become familiar with the system before implementing it on a large scale. Some popular digital platforms include the following.

- G Suite for Education (www.google.com/edu)
- Apple Education (www.apple.com/education)
- Microsoft Education (www.microsoft.com/en-us/education)

Even with a good digital platform in place, teaching today using digital devices is a challenge without also using a learning management system. These systems make it possible for teachers to better communicate, organize, and exchange digital files, including assignment files, with students. For example, a teacher can issue an assignment to students and then accept the completed assignment without the need to print documents. Students can also share and review assignments with their peers. Most schools and districts select one standard LMS so that students will not need to learn a different platform in each class. There are thousands of LMS platforms available, including the following.

- PowerSchool Learning (www.powerschool.com/solutions/lms)
- Otus (http://otus.com)
- Edmodo (http://edmodo.com)
- Canvas K–12 (http://canvaslms.com)

- Schoology (http://schoology.com)
- Google Classroom (http://classroom.google.com)

Defining and Deploying Financial Resources

At this early phase, as with the early visioning process discussed in chapter 1, conversations around financing the specific staff and technology resources your plan requires should include building and district leadership, as well as any other stakeholders that change or realignment might impact. If additional staff need to be hired to support the implementation, it's important to perform a financial evaluation to make sure that the budget can accommodate additional or reassigned staff. In many districts, this budgeting phase may take place over several years, depending on a building or department's specific needs.

Making a good plan that covers the immediate implementation costs of your vision, as well as its long-term budget, is vital to its success. Every district's needs and resources will be unique. You will want to work closely with all the stakeholders to create an implementation plan and budget. The question of whether to buy or lease equipment can be particularly crucial; many initial technology needs, such as adding wireless access points, upgrading cables, or purchasing new devices, can be big-ticket budget items. Many districts find that leasing provides a way to keep devices current while limiting expenses, and your business office should be aware that this is an option.

Once the staff infrastructure is in place, the team should select devices for students that fit within the budget allocation. Deployment decisions may include all the logistics from ordering these devices to actually getting them into the hands of students. Each school in the district should be involved in planning for this successful equipment rollout.

You should charge the business office and technology department with these budget issues, as well as with an evaluation of any costs associated with software subscriptions, Internet filtering, or other such issues with financing technology improvements. Beyond specific software subscriptions and devices, the budgeting process also needs to include potential investments in infrastructure. For example, most technology innovations will require robust Wi-Fi access in all parts of the building to be successful, and you may need to perform an access study to identify the required equipment and whether the building's construction can support it. Unless your district is large enough to have multiple technology leaders on staff such as network and system administrators, you may want to contract an access study. Many small districts look to vendors for conducting this type of analysis as few have these types of specialists employed.

Conclusion

In summary, success greatly depends on the amount of careful planning that takes place up front. Much as *location, location, location* determines a property's value, *planning, planning, planning* will largely contribute to the value add for your innovation.

Remember to think outside the box when determining new roles needed within a restrictive budget; often a redefinition of existing roles can meet the innovation's needs without employing additional personnel.

Just as students' learning needs to be differentiated, so too, does the adults' learning. Differentiate based on feedback, then scaffold and support each individual's journey. Provide a reference manual of where help can be obtained, depending on the issue or question.

Plan carefully for the platform and learning management system. Involve the business office in budgeting for the innovation and develop both short- and long-range needs. Try to stick to the plan within reason so that the board will be confident in endorsing the financial resources needed for success.

DISCUSSION QUESTIONS

Consider the following questions for personal reflection or in collaborative work with colleagues.

▶ In your school district, what are some of the resources your team will need to discuss as part of this innovation?

▶ What type of technology is currently accessible? How could some of that equipment be moved or repurposed?

▶ What is the current state of your building infrastructure, including Wi-Fi access?

▶ Why is it important to select a digital platform that is the same across the district?

▶ What is an example of a collaborative learning platform, and what, if anything, does your school already use?

▶ What changes might you need to make in staff roles to support deployment?

▶ How will the budget support the planned initiative?

▶ What type of devices do you believe would be best for teaching and learning in your building, and why?

▶ Which stakeholders in your school or district might try to block the innovation, and why? How might you convince them not to do this?

▶ Will this innovation, when complete, require you to make other technology changes? What might those be?

The *Then What*: Providing Professional Development and Sharing Your Story

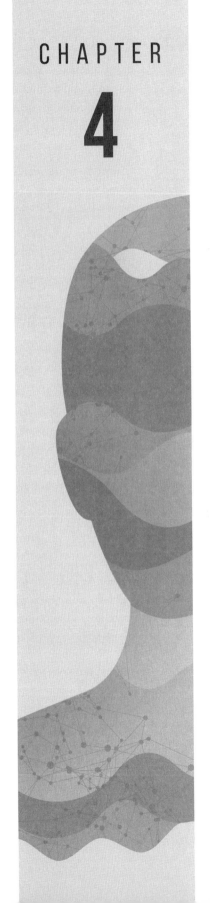

No device or innovation alone can change the culture of a school or district; real change comes with hard work over time. This leads us to a question: Once you roll out your vision, then what do you do to sustain it and continue its growth? In this chapter, we look at some answers to this question, with a specific focus on professional development and the concept of getting it out the door, or continually communicating student work outside the school or district in order to plant seeds of innovation in the community as well as other districts.

Professional Development

Traditionally, professional development was an event that took place on only a few days in each year, and that remained, as a rule, completely disconnected from the specific personal needs of classroom teachers. Often administrators hired an outside expert to guide teachers through presentation slides that presented new ideas. A few teachers might use one or two of these, but such changes were generally short-lived. As a result, schools experienced isolated pockets of improvement but no systemic change.

This type of one-and-done professional development session doesn't work because it doesn't operate according to an understanding of how adults—and more specifically, teachers—actually learn. Michael Fullan (2008), a thought leader in educational research and former dean of the Ontario Institute for Studies in Education, created a concept called the *six secrets of change*. The six secrets are: (1) love your employees, (2) connect peers with purpose, (3) build capacity, (4) learning is the work, (5) transparency rules, and (6) systems learn.

Among these secrets of change are two that relate to NOW classrooms and professional development: (1) build capacity and (2) connect peers with purpose. These change secrets Fullan (2008) writes about are simple in theory, but they're important tools to use when trying to establish ongoing and differentiated professional development that will further your innovation's success over time. Most important, Fullan (2008) promotes the idea that everyone in school should be engaged in supportive and ongoing active learning—not just teachers but also students. According to this thinking, any real change in schools needs to start with a small, committed group of teachers who are ready to try new instructional strategies using technology tools.

The ongoing, job-embedded professional development Fullan (2008) advocates is replete with benefits. As Hayes Mizell (2010) states:

> Professional development yields three levels of results: (a) educators learn new knowledge and skills because of their participation; (b) educators use what they learn to improve teaching and leadership; and (c) student learning and achievement increase because educators use what they learned in professional development. (p. 16)

When thinking about effective professional development, remember the idea of growth mindsets we wrote about in chapter 1. We know that, given the needed time and support, all students are capable of learning; growth mindset research indicates that teachers are, as well. Marie Clay, originator of the Reading Recovery (https://reading recovery.org) intervention, often referred to educators as green and growing or ripe and rotten. As leaders, we are responsible for providing experiences and opportunities that will help staff remain green and growing. This means making proper use of instructional coaches, understanding the principal's role, establishing personal learning networks, and supplementing professional development with effective social media use.

Instructional Coaches

Instructional coaches work with teachers to further develop their skills or to teach them new ones altogether. Using coaches also helps ensure that teachers have direct, consistent, and job-embedded professional development that aligns with their specific needs.

Instructional coaches also help teachers plan to integrate technology into their curriculum, with the goal of helping to develop more above-the-line student learning in the classroom (see the discussion of the SAMR model in chapter 1). Another positive effect of using instructional coaches is to build capacity by creating teacher leaders. Coaches empower teachers to take risks and to share what they've learned with their peers, helping to propel innovative practices across grade-level teams or schools.

The ultimate goal for each instructional coach is to regularly work with a small number of teachers, although initially finances may cause instructional coaches to be stretched thin, serving multiple buildings. For example, in the 2015–2016 school year, coaches in Berwyn South School District 100 worked with five to seven teachers in each of the two buildings they were assigned to, spanning a 330-plus teacher district. Despite such logistical hurdles, however, the instructional coach model is powerful and has gained traction. A key component of a successful coaching partnership is establishing a clear goal. This helps to drive the work and defines when the partnership is complete. Once a teacher has met her goal with integration and is able to apply the new skill independently, the instructional coach can move on to a new partnership, allowing other teachers in the school to receive support.

Instructional coaches work across all schools to bring teachers *above the line* on the SAMR model, moving from substitution and augmentation to modification and redefinition. Coaches can use a variety of approaches, including co-planning, modeling of instruction, and sharing curated resources. The goal is to support teachers in increasing student engagement and learning while leveraging technology resources.

The Role of the Principal

The building principal is critical to supporting professional development efforts. In fact, the building principal's leadership practices are one of the best predictors of success during a technology rollout. To ensure that teachers are on board with the process, the principal should clearly state the school's professional development goals. These goals should initially be shared verbally and then be provided in writing, perhaps in the school improvement plan or the professional development plan, for future reference. Creating a video of the initial verbal sharing can also provide a helpful future reference tool. School goals should be relevant to the school's specific situation but should also reflect the district's overall vision, just as individual teacher goals reflect school goals. Learning to set such goals—and learning to craft them to take advantage of specific teachers' expertise, when possible—is the most important first step a principal can take toward change. The principal should also provide teachers with an outlined plan for achieving these goals. If the teachers know what is expected of them, then the professional development will be more successful.

The following six questions can be helpful when formulating and refining these school goals.

1. Are the goals specific and achievable?

2. Do they support good instruction?

3. Do they allow for growth at all levels of understanding?

4. Do the learning opportunities the school plans connect to these goals?

5. Does the school's plan for assessing whether teachers have achieved their professional development goals relate well with the school's instructional model?

6. Do learning opportunities promote practice, retention, and application?

During professional development itself, the principal should offer feedback to help make positive changes in teachers' instruction and to benefit student learning. Depending on the type of feedback, it may be provided verbally in person as a part of a conversation or in writing with an invitation for follow-up if the teacher would like. At the end of each year, the principal should help teachers set clear, focused, and measurable goals for the following year based on data about the previous year, as well as on focused feedback from staff and other stakeholders. Many teacher evaluation processes include a formal goal setting process which can incorporate this idea.

The principal can also foster professional development in other ways. For example, a principal might offer personalized support to those who need it, such as a series of lunch and learns, a summer boot camp, extra time with an instructional coach, a system of learning buddies, an afterschool workshop, or help from a peer. Staff participating in these opportunities should have a clear goal for their learning in mind to create a purposeful experience with clear next steps. Following the learning experiences, the staff should be prepared to practice their skills and apply what they have learned. All such personalized learning activities should be tailored to individual staff members' needs to help them meet specific, measurable goals. Meeting teachers' needs in this way is one of the most important jobs a building principal can do, but it can also be a point of frustration. Leaders know the culture of their buildings and whether or not adequate time for learning is available during the day. What works in one district may not be successful in another. Consider the use of learning lunches to support specific goals throughout the year. Lunch is one of the few times of the day when teachers are available to meet without students and, if the culture permits, it can be quite successful. In some districts, however, this time may not be well received and teachers may choose not to attend. If learning lunches are considered, be sure that there is adequate time provided throughout the remainder of the day for other planning and learning. When facing a situation like this, it can be helpful for a principal to go back to the specific goals established during the early phases of the innovation and to engage in a professional conversation with staff regarding expectations and soliciting input as to when learning will best be received.

Personal Learning Networks

Every day, teachers can engage in meaningful professional dialogue with other teachers in their building and with their building principal. But although 21st century teachers have unlimited access to digital information, they are sometimes hard-pressed for time to collaborate with colleagues in their own buildings, let alone others in the profession.

One solution to this problem is to encourage teachers to develop an effective personal learning network (PLN). There are many different definitions for a PLN, including this explanation from the *Shift* blog (Gutierrez, 2016):

> Your PLN is where you gather, collect, communicate, create and also share knowledge and experience with a group of connected people, anywhere at any time. It is developed largely through social media, such as Twitter, LinkedIn, Facebook, and blogs, helping us form connections, grow our knowledge base and develop ourselves professionally through continual learning.

We created our own PLN in the course of collaborating on this book. Our PLN served as the glue that kept us connected throughout our work together on the five books in this series, and we also find it to be a good model for teachers who want to support their professional development. To create a PLN, users need an Internet-connected device and a social media account such as one on Twitter. Once the account is created, school leaders can connect with other educators. A good way to start connecting with other educators is to follow the hashtags #edchat or #suptchat and follow people participating in the conversations about education.

Focused feedback is critical to the success of any learning innovation, and teachers can and should use their PLNs to generate that feedback. A PLN can discuss the innovation results within the classroom, supporting that discussion with data they collect through formative and summative assessments, in order to determine what works or doesn't work about their practices and to strategize about potential solutions. The PLN can then coordinate as a group with the building principal and colleagues to make any necessary changes in the implementation of the vision.

Teachers on a professional development journey using technology can also work with other teachers near and far by using social media to share their discoveries. One way to demonstrate what they are learning and doing is by sharing the work their students are doing. We find that asking teachers to share student work—particularly on Twitter using the district hashtag or via digital portfolios—encourages them to continue their personal professional development, as well as dialogue and collaboration between colleagues that lasts beyond the school day.

Professional Development Through Social Media

Our writing team uses Twitter for personal professional development, and other PLNs should consider doing the same. Many of the authors of this book participate in and lead Twitter chats, organized by specific hashtags that focus on school leadership. For example, you might organize a chat around one of the following hashtags: #edchat, #growthmindset, #futureready, #suptchat, or #NOWClassrooms. These chats are usually weekly or biweekly, and each thirty- to sixty-minute chat has a specific focus. Usually the chat leader creates a series of questions for participants to respond to. Asking your teachers and staff to participate in such chats within their PLNs—or participating in them yourself!—can be an effective way to share ideas beyond geographic boundaries. In addition to Twitter, we often use YouTube to become familiar with new websites or apps. A quick search on the video platform can save hours of independent research. YouTube also has a social component in that viewers can comment on the videos directly on the site.

Connecting With the Community and Showcasing Student Work

One of the key themes of this series of books is the importance of telling your school's story of student engagement beyond the walls of the school or district. We refer to this as *getting it out the door*, with *it* being student projects that include the four Cs of communication, collaboration, critical thinking, and creativity (Partnership for 21st Century Learning, 2015). It takes higher-level thinking about a concept to teach it to someone else in a creative way, and we want students to exhibit that thinking by creating all types of artifacts that they share beyond classroom walls.

Some of these student products could include:

- Filming a movie
- Designing and recording a screencast
- Recording a podcast
- Creating a three-dimensional representation
- Researching and creating an infographic
- Creating a piece of mashup media
- Directing and recording a play
- Writing and recording a song
- Broadcasting a message using multimedia

There are many more ideas. (See appendix A [page 49] for an overview of projects within the grade-band books that teachers can use to bring these ideas into the classroom.) Try to engage students as ambassadors of the vision right from the start, as early as the pilot program, and provide evidence of your innovation's success outside of school or district walls. The following sections detail some platforms you can use to share student work, including Seesaw, social media, and traditional channels.

Seesaw

Parents love to see their children engaged and excited about school, and the free app Seesaw (http://web.seesaw.me) is an effective way for teachers to reach them. Seesaw allows teachers to create student-driven digital portfolios on any Internet-enabled device with the Google Chrome browser installed. Once the teacher sets up a class account, the intuitive app allows students to create, snap, and share what they create. Once the teacher approves the project, families can instantly see and comment on their child's creations.

As a writing team, we have watched Seesaw in action in our classrooms. *Wow* seriously understates the degree to which it helped us do our jobs as instructional leaders. The progress of Seesaw through our districts almost serves as a model for a successful innovation rollout; a few tech-savvy teachers in some of our buildings started the movement, and as teacher leaders, they brought their grade-level teams along to try out Seesaw. Soon, when teachers were considering trying out a new activity, the standard question became "Is this activity Seesaw worthy or not?"

Here are some of the reasons we've seen that people rave about Seesaw.

- Parents rave about the great communication between home and school.

- Teachers love Seesaw because the app makes it easy for even the youngest learners, such as kindergarteners, to share their work and learning with their parents.

- Administrators love the premium upgrade, which lets them pull reports from all the teachers in the building to document partnership connections between home and school.

- Central office personnel love Seesaw because leaders can finally monitor how technology is being used in classrooms.

- Most important, students feel empowered to capture and share what they have created with a broader and more authentic audience.

Building administrators can start with the free version of Seesaw to encourage teachers to use it and to spread the excitement from classroom to classroom. The premium version adds the ability to save student work from year to year in a portfolio. This creates a unique, cool graduation gift for students to take with them when they leave your building—as well as a good way to help administrators, parents, and district leadership study a student's overall learning progression.

Social Media

Just as Seesaw tells the story of a classroom, social media platforms such as Facebook and Twitter tell the story of a building or district. Therefore, encourage teachers to use classroom accounts to send out photos of student work that involve the four Cs (Partnership for 21st Century Learning, 2015) using the building or district hashtag.

Broadcasting classroom projects over Twitter hashtags not only helps the district tell its story but also helps teachers rethink what students are doing in the classroom. Just as teachers in our district began to ask themselves, "Is this activity Seesaw worthy?" teachers who used Twitter hashtags over time began to describe rote projects as "not really Twitter worthy." Snapping a picture of a worksheet is rarely what the district Twitter feed is looking for, and teachers who want to put a spotlight on their classrooms start to change their approach.

The greatest advantage of using social media, of course, is that students become highly engaged with it. Students frequently ask teachers to tweet out pictures of assignments and then let them know how many times the post was retweeted. Often, students can be heard discussing how to best share projects or pictures using their iPads. They know they are capable of getting information out beyond their classroom walls and are proud to share their work with others. This sometimes extends beyond the community, the state, and even the country. For example, they might use a platform they've utilized to communicate locally with parents and teachers, and then ask their teacher to tweet their work in the hopes that it will travel many miles.

This strategy doesn't just apply for the big social media platforms; consider also using the school website to show learning in action, or creating a kiosk outside the school office where you loop images from the district hashtag of the four Cs in action. This last strategy communicates your vision's importance not just outside the building but inside as well. Soon, the teachers who are slow to incorporate the four Cs into lessons will notice that their students are not the superstars of the photo stream. Again, a little constructive peer pressure online can lead to changed instructional practice.

Traditional Channels

Despite these new technologies, it's important not to forget the classic forms of connecting schools to parents and other community stakeholders, including parent-teacher association (PTA) or board meetings. One particularly effective tactic for using these events is to invite students to them to present their projects. This has multiple payoffs: it encourages the students to become better speakers and presenters, and it also brings parents and community members to the meetings to see their children in action. (Watching a first grader explain how he used a green screen to make a video at one such meeting was hilarious.) Such meetings typically have low attendance, and making use of student work, in addition to its other benefits, can be a good way to start bringing more parents and other community stakeholders into contact with the school.

Whatever channels of communication you and your staff prefer, the important thing is to get the message out the door and celebrate your successes! Communities want to see learning in action. (We do too; please feel free to share student work on our #NOWClassrooms Twitter hashtag. We can't wait to see what your students create.)

Conclusion

As much as possible, plan to embed professional development into the school day. Our personal experiences demonstrate that this real-time learning helps staff understand the integration of the innovation much more readily than separate trainings. Peers are often the best coaches, as working with a peer tends to reduce apprehension about risk taking, as compared to working with someone in an evaluative role.

It is important to clearly communicate goals and provide frequent feedback on growth toward those goals. Celebrations are confidence builders along the way. Try to choose readily achievable goals initially, to propel a natural desire to do more.

Encourage the use of PLNs and social media as support systems beyond the school or district. This is particularly important in small districts where there may only be one teacher of a grade level or subject.

Stay connected to the community and communicate frequently. Remember that many residents may not have children in the school system. It's imperative to reach everyone in the community for ongoing support of the innovation.

DISCUSSION QUESTIONS

Consider the following questions for personal reflection or in collaborative work with colleagues.

▸ What opportunities are currently available for ongoing professional development for all staff members?

▸ How does the professional development process build capacity in students, teachers, administrators, and parents?

▸ How do you communicate the process for professional development? What do you do to ensure that all stakeholders understand it?

▸ What do you believe is the key role of an instructional coach? What skills would you look for in hiring one?

▸ What are three things a building principal might do to encourage changes in teaching, learning, and technology?

▸ The idea of sharing student work beyond the walls of the classroom might push people outside of their comfort zone. Why might it be important to do this?

▸ What are three specific ways that your building or district can begin to showcase student work?

A Shifting Vision

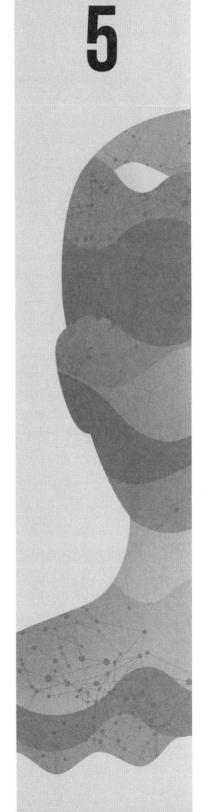

We are preparing our students for their future, not our past, and thus we must always remember that the ability to adapt is necessary for survival in the 21st century. According to Killion (2011), "To make substantive changes in teaching and learning, professional learning must be a continuous process sustained over a period of time that engages educators in learning from experts and with and from one another." A key understanding for success in any innovation is acknowledging that when moving forward, you will always need to make tweaks and adjustments. This concluding chapter deals with that process of rethinking and revision by examining change as a constant, assessing success, and looking ahead to the educational innovation's future.

Remembering That Change Is Constant

As technology advances, your team might find that a piece of equipment or software that was initially crucial to your innovation is no longer necessary. For example, a districtwide implementation of a tool such as G Suite for Education may eliminate the need for local servers, thus reducing the demand for electronic storage within buildings. This storage savings may even allow resources previously allocated to servers to be redirected to other learning innovation needs. A good implementation plan is responsive to these types of changes.

Other changes over time may involve the development of entirely new technologies that create the ability to share student work more easily in real time. For example, after Maercker School District 60's first year of implementing a learning innovation using school-owned Chromebooks in 2014, the district discovered Go Guardian. Go Guardian allows teachers to push out links to all students in real time, allowing lessons to be more tailored to student outcomes. It also provides teachers with a dashboard of the students' Chromebooks. The dashboard allows teachers to project the students' screens, enabling them to share their work and facilitating class discussions and feedback opportunities.

Occasionally, the required technology may not yet be available at an affordable price and leaders may be forced to move toward a determined vision without an optimal solution to a particular challenge. We encourage you to forge ahead and keep abreast of technology changes because often, within a few short months, prices will drop or a new platform, tool, or device will become available. New technology has the ability to change what is possible even while an implementation is in progress. To take advantage of developing technology, leaders can plan on making mid-course adjustments. Change is constant, and professional development to keep up with new opportunities will also need to be constant, seamless, and ongoing.

Assessing Success

Without good data to measure the success of your innovation, there's no effective way to revise it. In a modern world, data are ubiquitous, but there are several digital tools, ranging from free applications to paid solutions, to help you collect, organize, and ultimately make sense of the information available to you. G Suite for Education, for example, provides the following tools that you can use for data collection and management.

- Google Forms to collect data
- Google Docs to collaborate and brainstorm around data
- Google Drawing to visualize data
- Google Sheets to study data
- Google Slides to present data

Appendix B contains many more data-management tools, and we regularly share new tools on our collaborative blog (www.nowclassrooms.com). Additionally, some learning management systems, including Otus and Summit Learning, make a direct connection between data and personalized learning paths for students, an evolving trend known as *competency-based learning*. Competency-based learning involves a focus on students acquiring a specific set of defined skills. In a competency-based learning classroom, students have individual goals that they work on at their own pace while also working on small-group projects and whole-class activities.

Apart from data, students themselves should be a key information source about the success of an innovation. In theory, building and district leaders should be able to stop and ask student groups not only the purpose of a lesson they're engaged in but also what outside audience they are targeting. Students should also be able to articulate how teachers will assess their progress toward specific learning objectives. Such critical conversations with students can help a school leader understand how teachers have structured and presented lessons to students; if the teachers structure the lessons carefully, students will be comfortable answering your questions.

Using formative assessment to evaluate teaching and learning is just as important for students as it is for teachers. Based on the results of a quick formative assessment, teachers can modify the next day's instructional plan to better respond to students' needs. Traditional formative checking strategies such as individual student whiteboards, exit slips on paper, and pretests all continue to have a role in the classroom, supplemented by new technology to automate formative data collection. Some potential supplemental technology platforms include the following.

- Kahoot! (https://getkahoot.com)
- Formative (https://goformative.com)
- Plickers (www.plickers.com)
- Socrative (www.socrative.com)
- Quizizz (https://quizizz.com)
- Padlet (https://padlet.com)
- Quizlet (https://quizlet.com)

These are just a few formative assessment technology apps and websites you can share with your staff. As the school leader, at the start of every staff meeting, you might ask one staff member to engage his or her colleagues in a short formative assessment experience using one of these resources. This can be a great way to cultivate growth mindsets, encourage teacher leadership, and provide a short professional development session all at once.

Whatever tools and platforms you decide to use, remember one thing: change is constant. As building and district leaders, this can easily become a source of frustration. But it is also a natural part of working with teaching, learning, and technology. Innovation is not a one-and-done committee; planning and monitoring will continue for years, and as devices and products change, new conversations will occur among the planning team. Even as tools, devices, and apps change, however, the central part of the vision must remain: teaching and learning first, technology in their service.

Looking Ahead

We continue to learn every day from watching the changes in the world around us. Pockets of great teachers develop new instructional strategies that harmonize technology and a focus on the four Cs (Partnership for 21st Century Learning, 2015), and these teachers fill up our district hashtags with pictures of students engaged in their learning. Parents love the projects that their students create and share using Seesaw or on social media and have replaced the question, "What did you do in school today?" with a trip to the district Twitter hashtag to see what's going on in the classroom and then a more focused discussion at home—"Tell me all about that interesting project I saw you working on in your class Twitter feed!" These classrooms buzz with the excitement of students who collaborate with one another and drive their own learning.

On our way to peek into one of these engaged classrooms, however, we sometimes pass some rooms that have gone back to more traditional instructional methods. Some of these classrooms don't have the benefit of new technology, although some of them do and still rely on rote instruction. We know that systemic change is going to take years, and we know that the work of bringing about that change will lead us to revisit these topics again and again with different teacher groups. But we also know that some teachers are simply waiting for this trend in education to end so that they can go back to the way teaching and learning used to be.

We cannot allow this "close the door and do what I have always done" approach to stop our forward movement. Here's what's at stake: as we worked with our staff on the four Cs, we noticed a few things starting to happen in our classrooms, in our hallways, and in parent communications. We saw fewer bland projects where the teacher had directed exactly what the final product should look like: fewer dioramas all on the same topic, fewer posters all organized in the same way, fewer one-size-fits-all writing prompts, fewer cookie-cutter book reports, fewer worksheets, fewer default PowerPoint templates. Instead, we noticed an increase in student voice and choice as students created unique projects to share beyond the classroom's walls. We started to hear teachers in team meetings talk about how they could incorporate new technology into upcoming lessons. We started to hear teachers finally talk about giving up some of their treasured projects of the past and trying something new. We started to hear their excitement when the superintendent retweeted projects that students had created in their classrooms. We started to hear from parents that their sons and daughters now loved to come to school, where they could do work "like they do in the real world."

There's more. Some of our classroom teachers are using Google's translation tools to connect with families who speak a variety of languages. Printed newsletters are now outdated; in this age of acceleration, a picture says a thousand words, and we share those pictures every day. Grandparents have now become part of the mix on Facebook, and experts virtually visit classrooms on a regular basis. One grade level managed to bring a silviculturist from the National Park Service in Oregon to a professional development session held via Skype. (Go to goo.gl/wNI2y3 to check out the video.)

We have not reached every teacher—yet! A growth mindset teaches us that everyone changes at a different pace, and we still have many staff members to move. But we are encouraged to see less direct instruction and more students collaborating in groups using the four Cs (Partnership for 21st Century Learning, 2015). Most important, every day, instead of being bored and disengaged with rote assignments, our students and teachers are actively excited about what they're learning and sharing.

Conclusion

Throughout this leadership guide, we have shared our passion for creating learning environments that equip our students with the lifelong learning skills they need to be successful in a rapidly changing world. Starting with planning and visioning, we created a road map for school leaders to bring lasting change to their schools. Each of our journeys has taken a slightly different path, and so will your work because we are all starting from different points of readiness.

Although everyone's journey will be unique, we hope this book will serve as your guide to create highly engaged and digitally enriched 21st century classrooms. Following our lead in this guide, you are on the road to create change-focused schools that prepare students for the real world beyond school. We can't predict the jobs of the future but we know that the students of today will be the leaders of the future and they need the super skills of the four Cs—collaboration, creativity, critical thinking, and communication. These super skills need to be woven into the lessons in our classrooms today to prepare students for college and careers of the future.

Take this guide and your new growth mindset and get ready to tackle the challenges you will face as you move your staff, students, and community to a new future of teaching and learning. As you look to the future, please join our PLN, #NOWClassrooms, to see updates from our team and share your own successes.

DISCUSSION QUESTIONS

Consider the following questions for personal reflection or in collaborative work with colleagues.

▸ Where is your team in the process of creating a learning and technology innovation? Can you describe that innovation in a single paragraph?

▸ What is one specific example of something your team has had to rethink in response to new technology becoming available?

▸ What are some of the new products, apps, or platforms your team is currently looking at?

▸ How are you communicating your innovation to your community? Who is telling your story?

▸ As your community's learning culture shifts, what work do you still feel needs to be done?

▸ How might you incorporate formative assessment and technology at the classroom or building level?

▸ How might you use one of the solutions in this book to better use and interpret data?

▸ Based on the information in this chapter, can you create a checklist for assessing success in your setting?

▸ What are the next steps in your team's journey?

▸ After reading this book, what are three key ideas you will put into action?

Appendix A: Grade-Band Books at a Glance

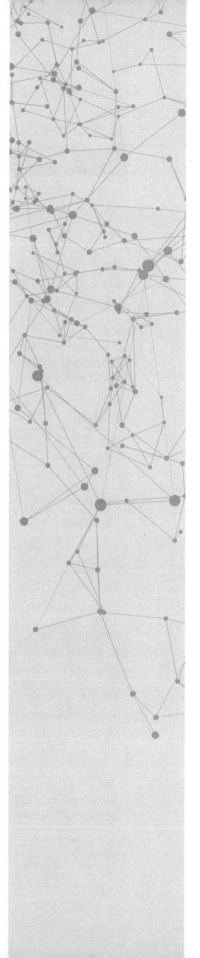

The tables in this appendix break down the NOW lessons found in each chapter in each grade-band book in the *NOW Classrooms* series.

Table A.1 lists the lessons found in *NOW Classrooms, Grades K–2*.

Table A.1: Lessons in *NOW Classrooms, Grades K–2*

Chapter 1: Learning Technology Operations and Concepts		
Learning Basic Operations and Troubleshooting		
Novice	**Operational**	**Wow**
Using Basic Keyboarding and Touch-Screen Navigation	Seeking Help From Peers to Solve a Technology Problem	Solving Technology Problems With Tech-Sperts
Introducing LMS Features to Students		
Novice	**Operational**	**Wow**
Getting Started With an LMS	Uploading Content to an LMS	Updating Existing LMS Content
Chapter 2: Embracing Creativity		
Snapping and Sharing Photos		
Novice	**Operational**	**Wow**
Taking Pictures With a Camera App	Sequencing Pictures	Demonstrating Learning Using Pictures
Recording and Sharing Videos		
Novice	**Operational**	**Wow**
Recording Videos	Creating a Video Project	Creating a Multimedia Movie
Recording and Sharing Audio		
Novice	**Operational**	**Wow**
Recording Audio Messages	Assessing Learning Using Audio	Using Audio to Teach Peers
Chapter 3: Communicating and Collaborating		
Using Video to Flip Learning		
Novice	**Operational**	**Wow**
Learning From Flipped Video Lessons	Creating a Flipped Video Lesson	Sharing a Flipped Video Lesson With Peers
Sharing With Social Media		
Novice	**Operational**	**Wow**
Creating and Sharing in a Digital Community	Connecting Classrooms Through a Digital Community	Connecting With an Authentic Audience Using Social Media

Establishing Live Local and Global Connections		
Novice	Operational	Wow
Giving Live Feedback to Other Students	Using Technology to Connect Outside the Classroom	Learning With a Live Global Audience

Chapter 4: Conducting Research and Curating Information		
Gathering and Evaluating Information		
Novice	Operational	Wow
Knowing the Difference Between Fiction and Nonfiction When Researching	Using Online Resources to Gather Information	Choosing Resources Independently

Chapter 5: Thinking Critically to Solve Problems		
Planning and Producing Using Digital Tools		
Novice	Operational	Wow
Learning About Digital Tools	Selecting Appropriate Digital Tools From a Menu	Independently Selecting a Digital Tool to Complete a Task
Managing Projects Independently		
Novice	Operational	Wow
Following Directions for a Multistep Digital Task	Completing a Multistep Task in a Small Group	Independently Sequencing a Multistep Task

Chapter 6: Being Responsible Digital Citizens		
Creating Digital Citizens		
Novice	Operational	Wow
Staying Safe Online	Protecting Personal Data From Strangers	Putting a Stop to Cyberbullying
Understanding Creative Work and Intellectual Property		
Novice	Operational	Wow
Labeling Work Online	Crediting the Work of Others	Citing Resources in Digital Projects

Chapter 7: Expanding Technology and Coding Concepts		
Coding for Everyone		
Novice	Operational	Wow
Understanding Basic Coding	Coding While Unplugged	Coding a Simple Toy

Table A.2 lists the lessons found in *NOW Classrooms, Grades 3–5*.

Table A.2: Lessons in *NOW Classrooms, Grades 3–5*

Chapter 1: Embracing Creativity		
Working With Digital Images		
Novice	**Operational**	**Wow**
Searching for Digital Images	Annotating Digital Photos	Enhancing Digital Photos
Creating Video Projects		
Novice	**Operational**	**Wow**
Creating Book Trailers	Creating Multimedia Projects With Photos or Video	Mashing Up Video, Photos, and Audio Into a Project
Working With Audio		
Novice	**Operational**	**Wow**
Recording My Thinking	Manipulating Multiple Audio Files	Engaging My Audience With Sound Effects
Creating Meaningful Multimedia Projects		
Novice	**Operational**	**Wow**
Using Visuals to Show My Learning	Finding the Best Way to Demonstrate My Learning	Annotating My Multimedia Presentation
Chapter 2: Communicating and Collaborating		
Creating and Using Instructional Videos		
Novice	**Operational**	**Wow**
Evaluating Instructional Videos	Creating an Instructional Video	Assisting Others' Learning With Instructional Videos
Connecting With a Variety of Audiences		
Novice	**Operational**	**Wow**
Connecting With Classmates	Connecting With Peers	Connecting With a Global Audience
Collaborating and Giving Feedback		
Novice	**Operational**	**Wow**
Giving and Receiving Feedback	Collaborating With Peers	Collaborating Globally

Chapter 3: Conducting Research and Curating Information		
Gathering Information		
Novice	**Operational**	**Wow**
Gathering Information From a List of Sources	Gathering Information Through a Familiar Website	Getting Information Through a Search Engine
Evaluating Information		
Novice	**Operational**	**Wow**
Identifying Aspects of a Reliable Source	Determining the Purpose of a Website	Identifying a Reliable Source
Chapter 4: Thinking Critically to Solve Problems		
Evaluating and Choosing Digital Tools		
Novice	**Operational**	**Wow**
Selecting Digital Tools	Defining the Properties of Digital Tools	Identifying the Right Tool for the Task
Planning and Managing Projects		
Novice	**Operational**	**Wow**
Planning, Managing, and Sharing Online	Communicating With Collaborative Tools to Solve a Problem	Designing and Collaborating With Others
Finding Data-Driven Solutions		
Novice	**Operational**	**Wow**
Collecting Data	Analyzing the Data	Finding the Solution
Chapter 5: Being Responsible Digital Citizens		
Ensuring Internet Safety		
Novice	**Operational**	**Wow**
Identifying Internet Safety Components	Explaining How to Stay Safe Online	Showing How to Stay Safe Online
Understanding Legal and Ethical Behaviors		
Novice	**Operational**	**Wow**
Citing Sources on a Page	Creating a List of Sources	Creating Hyperdocs
Managing One's Digital Footprint		
Novice	**Operational**	**Wow**
Explaining Why I Need to Protect Information Online	Creating a Positive Online Image	Explaining How My Digital Footprint Is Important

continued ▶

Chapter 6: Expanding Technology and Coding Concepts		
Understanding and Troubleshooting Basic Operations		
Novice	**Operational**	**Wow**
Operating the Device	Utilizing Shortcuts	Troubleshooting Device Problems
Storing, Sharing, and Managing Online Files		
Novice	**Operational**	**Wow**
Creating Online	Locating and Sharing Files	Managing and Organizing Files
Coding		
Novice	**Operational**	**Wow**
Recognizing Sequential Steps for Coding	Applying Coding Skills	Creating With Coding

Table A.3 lists the lessons found in *NOW Classrooms, Grades 6–8*.

Table A.3: Lessons in *NOW Classrooms, Grades 6-8*

Chapter 1: Embracing Creativity		
Creating Experiences Through Imagery		
Novice	**Operational**	**Wow**
Using Pictures in Projects	Annotating and Adding Links to Images	Going Places With a Green Screen
Using Video to Roll Out the Red Carpet		
Novice	**Operational**	**Wow**
Creating Simple Movies	Creating Movie Masterpieces	Creating an Augmented Reality
Engaging the Ear Using Audio		
Novice	**Operational**	**Wow**
Creating a Presentation With Audio	Mixing Audio Like a DJ	Creating and Publishing a Podcast
Applying Creativity in New Ways		
Novice	**Operational**	**Wow**
Creating a Screencast	Smashing Apps Together	Publishing Products for a Wider Audience

Chapter 2: Communicating and Collaborating		
Communicating More Dynamically		
Novice	**Operational**	**Wow**
Backchanneling to Broaden Communication	Learning In an Online Classroom	Communicating Globally Using Blogs
Collaborating Better Online		
Novice	**Operational**	**Wow**
Writing Helpful Notes	Providing Feedback From Afar	Collaborating With Live Video Chat
Chapter 3: Conducting Research and Curating Information		
Becoming Knowledge Constructors		
Novice	**Operational**	**Wow**
Improving Search Results	Using Advanced Search Techniques	Annotating Internet Research
Finding Credible Information		
Novice	**Operational**	**Wow**
Brainstorming What to Search For	Evaluating a Source's Key Characteristics	Understanding and Identifying Bias
Becoming Lifelong Learners		
Novice	**Operational**	**Wow**
Participating in Interactive Learning	Flipping a Lesson	Creating an Interactive Lesson
Chapter 4: Thinking Critically to Solve Problems		
Planning It Out		
Novice	**Operational**	**Wow**
Using Technology to Plan a Project	Connecting With Experts Outside the Classroom	Choosing the Right Tool for the Job
Using Video to Hone Learning		
Novice	**Operational**	**Wow**
Evaluating Videos	Following and Creating Playlists to Organize Videos	Publishing Video Projects Online
Becoming Data Analysts		
Novice	**Operational**	**Wow**
Collecting and Visualizing Data	Making Charts and Graphs With Data	Publishing Research

continued ▶

Chapter 5: Being Responsible Digital Citizens		
Understanding Internet Safety		
Novice	**Operational**	**Wow**
Tapping Cyberbullying Resources	Using Online Tools Safely	Communicating Professionally Online
Engaging in Legal and Ethical Behaviors Online		
Novice	**Operational**	**Wow**
Understanding the Importance of Citations	Searching for Copyright-Free Resources	Obtaining a Creative Commons License
Creating a Positive Digital Footprint		
Novice	**Operational**	**Wow**
Creating and Securing Passwords	Protecting Personal Information Online	Fostering a Positive Digital Footprint
Chapter 6: Expanding Technology and Coding Concepts		
Managing the Chaos of Technology		
Novice	**Operational**	**Wow**
Troubleshooting Tablets and Laptops	Organizing Files and Folders Online	Building a Digital Portfolio
Coding With Confidence		
Novice	**Operational**	**Wow**
Participating In the Hour of Code	Developing Coding Skills	Creating Functional Apps

Table A.4 lists the lessons found in *NOW Classrooms, Grades 9–12*.

Table A.4: Lessons in *NOW Classrooms, Grades 9–12*

Chapter 1: Embracing Creativity		
Using Digital Images in Projects		
Novice	**Operational**	**Wow**
Explaining Ideas With Images	Creating Original Images	Annotating and Enhancing Images
Using Video to Demonstrate Learning		
Novice	**Operational**	**Wow**
Recording Short Videos	Editing to Improve Videos	Mashing Up Multimedia Assets

Using Audio to Enhance Understanding		
Novice	**Operational**	**Wow**
Proving Mastery Through Spoken Audio	Pairing Audio With Animated Elements	Producing Collaborative Audio
Combining Multimedia Elements to Create Effective Presentations		
Novice	**Operational**	**Wow**
Creating Simple Presentations	Creating More Dynamic Presentations	Creating True Multimedia Presentations
Chapter 2: Communicating and Collaborating		
Using Flipped Video to Communicate and Enhance Learning		
Novice	**Operational**	**Wow**
Evaluating Educational Videos	Creating Flipped Videos	Collaborating to Create and Evaluate Flipped Videos
Using Social Networking to Work as a Group		
Novice	**Operational**	**Wow**
Conversing Using Social Media	Using Social Media to Connect With a Broader Audience	Moderating Discussions on Social Media
Collaborating Online Using Live Communications		
Novice	**Operational**	**Wow**
Conducting Live Chats With Other Classrooms	Collaborating With Subject-Area Experts	Collaborating to Investigate and Solve Global Issues
Chapter 3: Conducting Research and Curating Information		
Gathering Information		
Novice	**Operational**	**Wow**
Gathering Preliminary Research	Gathering Information Using Advanced Searches	Analyzing Research
Evaluating Information		
Novice	**Operational**	**Wow**
Evaluating a Source's Usefulness	Determining a Source's Reliability	Determining a Source's Scholarliness

continued ▶

Chapter 4: Thinking Critically to Solve Problems		
Identifying and Defining Tasks for Investigation		
Novice	Operational	Wow
Solving Problems in the Classroom	Solving Problems Outside the Classroom	Publishing Solutions to Problems
Planning and Managing Projects		
Novice	Operational	Wow
Managing Time With Calendars	Managing Group Projects Outside the Classroom	Connecting With Experts
Collecting, Analyzing, and Presenting Data		
Novice	Operational	Wow
Collecting Data	Analyzing Data	Publishing and Presenting Data
Chapter 5: Being Responsible Digital Citizens		
Protecting Oneself and Others Online		
Novice	Operational	Wow
Evaluating a Website's Fine Print	Fostering Your Digital Footprint	Educating Others About Internet Safety
Engaging in Legal and Ethical Behaviors		
Novice	Operational	Wow
Identifying Different Kinds of Copyright	Avoiding Plagiarism and Citing Sources	Understanding Fair Use and Creating Licenses
Chapter 6: Expanding Technology and Coding Concepts		
Showcasing Work Online		
Novice	Operational	Wow
Safeguarding Work Online	Creating Digital Portfolios	Creating Video-Based Portfolios
Managing and Troubleshooting Devices		
Novice	Operational	Wow
Troubleshooting Devices	Making Better Use of Devices	Increasing Presentation Skills With Screen Sharing
Coding and Developing Applications		
Novice	Operational	Wow
Learning the Basics of Computer Coding	Developing Coding Skills	Building Functional Apps

Appendix B: Glossary of Tools and Terms

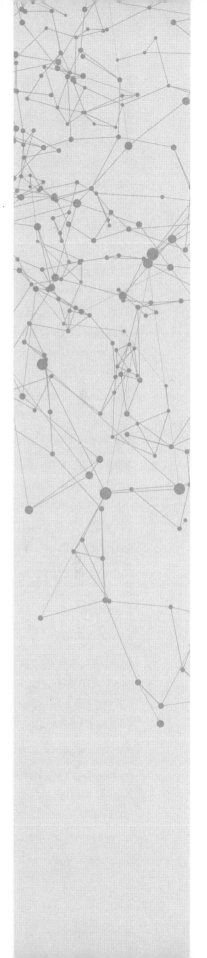

This appendix contains a list of technology tools, apps, websites, and terminology that we use throughout the *NOW Classrooms* series. A similar appendix appears in all the grade-band books. Your staff will find these definitions helpful as they learn about the many tools and apps discussed in the books.

Many of these apps and websites are free. Some have premium features that require a subscription; these are noted where applicable. Be sure to check a website's terms of service, as they are subject to change.

1:1 or one to one: Describes the number of technology devices (iPads, laptops, Chromebooks) given to each student in an academic setting; a 1:1 school has one device per each student

1:2 or one to two: Describes the number of technology devices (iPads, laptops, Chromebooks) given to each student in an academic setting; a 1:2 school means that one technology device is available for every two students in an academic setting; two classes may share one class set, or students may partner up to use devices

10 Frame Fill (www.classroomfocusedsoftware.com/10framefill.html): A mathematics app that uses the ten-frame concept with drag-and-drop manipulatives

ABCya (www.abcya.com): An educational app with games for students pre K through fifth grade

ABC—Magnetic Alphabet Lite for Kids (https://itunes.apple.com/us/app/abc -magnetic-alphabet-lite-for-kids/id389132393?mt=8): An app reminiscent of a chalkboard that uses virtual magnetic letters that students can manipulate into any configuration

About.me (https://about.me): An easy-to-use website that allows students to create a webpage with a unique link that highlights an important part of their web presence

Academic Kids (http://academickids.com): A free online encyclopedia for students

Adobe Spark (https://spark.adobe.com): A free website for designing graphics, images, videos, and webpages, with templates that make it easy for teachers and students to create projects

anchor chart: A chart for making thinking visible during the learning process while recording strategies, processes, guidelines, and other content

Animoto (https://animoto.com): A video-creation website and app with limited free features and options for educator accounts (see https://animoto.com/education /classroom)

app smashing: The process of using multiple apps to create projects or complete tasks

AppyPie (www.appypie.com): A free do-it-yourself software tool for building apps in three easy steps

ArtStudio (www.luckyclan.com): An app that includes a sketching, drawing, and photo editing tool

Asana (https://asana.com): A platform for managing and tracking large group projects

Ask a Tech Teacher (askatechteacher.com/2014/11/18/hour-of-code): A site with K–8 Hour of Code suggestions organized by grade level

Audacity (www.audacityteam.org): Free software for a Mac or Windows computer that makes editing complex audio clips possible

Audioboom (https://audioboom.com): A free resource to share audio content

augmented reality: Technology that uses the real world as a backdrop to computer-generated images; for example, Pokémon Go

Aurasma (www.aurasma.com): An augmented reality iOS and Android app that allows users to turn images or everyday objects into interactive experiences

AutoRap (www.smule.com/apps): An iOS and Android app for mixing audio tracks to create a rap; the free version allows you to choose from two beats to make a song and the paid version allows you to choose from a large selection of beats, including new and popular songs

Awwapp (www.awwapp.com): A touch-friendly online whiteboard app that lets you use your computer, tablet, or smartphone to easily draw sketches and collaborate with others

A–Z Animals (http://a-z-animals.com): An online encyclopedia with information about a huge variety of animals

backchannel: A place where groups of students can digitally comment to one another while observing a specific event

Bee-Bot (www.bee-bot.us): An introductory coding toy for elementary students

Big Brown Bear Keyboarding (www.bigbrownbear.co.uk/keyboard): A simple website for learning beginning keyboarding skills

Bing (www.bing.com): A Microsoft-developed search engine

Bitly (https://bitly.com): A tool for shortening URLs to make it easier for people to reach specific webpages

BitsBox (https://bitsbox.com): A subscription service that sends homes or schools monthly coding project kits

Blabberize (http://blabberize.com/): A website that mixes together an uploaded picture and recorded speech to make it seem like the picture is talking

Blackboard (www.blackboard.com): A learning management system that is fee based and often used at the higher education level

Blogger (www.blogger.com): Google's free, easy-to-use online blogging platform, packed with features, including the ability to leave comments for a blog's author

Bloglovin' (www.bloglovin.com): An app that consolidates many different blogs in one place; students can follow specific blogs and discover new ones

Book Creator (https://bookcreator.com): A tool available on the web or as an app for creating ebooks on iPads, Android tablets, and Windows tablets

BookFlix (www.scholastic.com/digital/bookflix.htm): A digital resource that pairs fictional video stories with nonfiction ebooks

Boolean operators: Simple words (AND, OR, NOT, or AND NOT) used to combine or exclude search terms in order to make a web search narrower or broader (see https://library.alliant.edu/screens/boolean.pdf)

Botlogic.us (http://botlogic.us): A web-based puzzle that teaches coding concepts

Bounce (www.bounceapp.com): A website where students can add notes to a screenshot of a webpage; there is no sign-on required, so annotated page links must be saved in another location

BrainPOP (www.brainpop.com): An animated educational site for students filled with short educational videos, including free content and paid subscription access for schools and districts

BrainPOP Jr. (https://jr.brainpop.com): A website that features short, animated educational videos for students in grades K–3 that also includes quizzes and related materials

Britannica School (www.school.eb.com): A paid subscription database that contains credible, searchable information in the form of web pages, journal articles, videos, and images

camera app: The app found on most portable devices that gives access to its camera for taking photos or recording video

Canva (www.canva.com): A website with free and premium features to create stunning graphics and visual content

Canvas K–12 (www.canvaslms.com/k-12): An LMS software tool for organizing students' digital work and managing, tracking, and reporting educational data and courses

ccMixter (http://ccmixter.org): A platform where people can take original music or voice samples and remix them into new songs

ChatterPix Kids (www.duckduckmoose.com/educational-iphone-itouch-apps -for-kids/chatterpixkids): An iPad- and iPhone-only app that students can use to record their voice, select a picture to attach the recording to, and play the recording back as if the object says what the students recorded

chatzy (www.chatzy.com): A platform for creating and joining private chat rooms

Chirbit (www.chirbit.com): An app and website that allows users to record voice memos and export voice memos as QR codes or as social media posts

Chrome (www.google.com/chrome): A web browser developed by Google that you can use on any device and that has additional features such as extensions and the ability to sync bookmarks across all devices

Citation Machine (www.citationmachine.net): A free online resource used to cite sources, step-by-step, in MLA, APA, and Chicago style formats

Classkick (www.classkick.com): An app that allows teachers to see what students are working on in real time on individual, Internet-connected devices

cloud computing: The practice of using a network of remote, Internet-hosted servers to store, manage, and process data

Codecademy (www.codecademy.com): A free website that helps anyone learn how to code; starting with the basics, students can learn a variety of programming languages

CodeCombat (https://codecombat.com): A web-gaming tool for learning programming

Code.org (https://code.org): A website for learning coding and programming on iPads, Chromebooks, and Android devices

Comic Life (http://plasq.com/apps/comiclife/macwin): A plasq-developed MacOS, iOS, and Windows comic desktop app that uses digital photos to create comic pages

Common Sense (www.commonsense.org): A collection of articles, videos, and resources to use for teaching digital citizenship; connects with offshoots Common Sense Media (www.commonsensemedia.org) and Common Sense Education (www.commonsense.org/education)

Creative Commons (https://creativecommons.org): An organization that offers various types of flexible copyrights that allow people to more easily share, use, and remix photo, video, and other creative content; each content item lists its usage rights, including whether it can be freely shared or modified and if attribution needs to be given when used

Crunchzilla (www.crunchzilla.com): A website that offers interactive tutorials to teach coding

D2L (www.d2l.com): A learning management system from Brightspace, short for Desire2Learn

Daisy the Dinosaur (www.daisythedinosaur.com): An introductory coding app

Daqri apps (https://daqri.com): An app series for iOS and Android devices students can use to view augmented reality content and complete activities on a variety of topics as well as play games and interact with works of art; apps in the suite include Elements 4D (http://elements4d.daqri.com/), Anatomy 4D (http://anatomy4d.daqri.com/), Enchantium, Crayola Color Alive (www.crayola.com/splash/products/ColorAlive), and Crayola Easy Animation (www.crayola.com/easyanimationstudio)

Dash and Dot (www.makewonder.com): Programmable robots with an app that utilizes block programming to help teach students how to code

Dashlane (www.dashlane.com): A program that generates passwords and stores them in one place; there are free and paid versions

DevArt (https://devart.withgoogle.com): Art made with code; students can view art and feel inspired to create their own

DHMO.org (www.dhmo.org): A hoax website that details the dangerous compound dihydrogen monoxide (water) and is commonly used to get students to think about source reliability

Digital Compass (www.digitalcompass.org): An app created through Common Sense Media for grades 6–8 to help students navigate the Internet safely

Digital Passport (www.digitalpassport.org): An app created through Common Sense Media for grades 3–5 to help students navigate through different resources about digital citizenship and Internet safety

Diigo (www.diigo.com): A social bookmarking tool for Chrome, iOS, and Android that lets users save, annotate, highlight, and share websites

DinoSearch (www.dinosearch.com): A safe search engine for students

Do Ink (www.doink.com): An iPad- and iPhone-only app for creating green-screen videos that has free features as well as premium features

Dotstorming (https://dotstorming.com): A free app groups can use to vote online through their own Dotstorming board

Dropbox (www.dropbox.com): A free service for storing and sharing files

Easel.ly (www.easel.ly): A template-based website with free and premium features for easily creating stunning infographics

EasyBib (www.easybib.com): A website and app for easily creating citations, with free options as well as premium features

Edge (www.microsoft.com/en-us/windows/microsoft-edge): A web browser developed by Microsoft that has replaced Internet Explorer

Edmodo (www.edmodo.com): One of the many learning management systems available

EDPuzzle (https://edpuzzle.com): A free website that allows teachers to choose various educational videos and insert comments and questions to gauge student understanding; after students complete lessons, teachers can review results

Educreations (www.educreations.com): An interactive, screencast whiteboard with free and premium options that students can use to record their learning

Edutopia (www.edutopia.org/topic/coding-classroom): A coding and programming website with discussions, articles, and other resources

Encyclopaedia Britannica (www.britannica.com): A free online encyclopedia

Encyclopedia.com (www.encyclopedia.com): A tool for gathering research and information

Epals (www.epals.com): An online global community in which you can connect with classrooms around the world and establish pen pal relationships or participate in global challenges

Epic! (www.getepic.com): A website and app that provides students with a digital library of high-interest books

EPUB (http://idpf.org/epub): A format for publishing and reading electronic books

Evernote (https://evernote.com): A web- and app-based note-taking and organization tool in which users can sync notes between devices and share and edit notes with others

Explain Everything (https://explaineverything.com): A paid collaborative and interactive whiteboard website and app for Android and Apple devices as well as a Google Chrome extension

Exploratorium (www.exploratorium.edu): A website with educational tools that the Exploratorium science museum in San Francisco, California, maintains

Facebook (www.facebook.com): A social media network to connect with others using text and pictures, either for professional or personal use, for those age thirteen or older

FaceTime (https://itunes.apple.com/us/app/facetime/id414307850?mt=12): A video telephone and video chat service for conducting one-on-one video calls among Apple devices

Flickr (www.flickr.com): A free website for searching for images that includes Explore functions and a Creative Commons category with images in the public domain

Flipagram (https://flipagram.com): An app that allows users to create short video stories with photos, video, and music

flipped learning: A learning model where the traditional classroom work-homework model is flipped—students watch video lectures at home and work on exercises, projects, and discussions in class

Fluency Tutor (https://fluency.texthelp.com/Chrome/Get): An extension in Google Chrome that you need to add to student devices to record students as they read on a computer or tablet

Fodey (www.fodey.com): A website with various templates that generate products for download, such as newspaper stories, movie clapper boards, cartoons, and more

Formative (https://goformative.com): A free website for collecting information in the form of a drawing, text, or multiple-choice response for a quick formative assessment that gives immediate individual feedback to students

Freerange (https://freerangestock.com): A website that offers free high-resolution stock images and textures

G Suite for Education (www.google.com/intl/en_us/edu/): An overarching term for all the Google products that a school system has available for staff and student use

GarageBand (www.apple.com/mac/garageband): Apple-only software and an iPad and iPhone app for making music, recording narrations, and creating new audio projects

Genius Hour: Time set aside for students to research and learn about whatever interests them

Genius Hour Blog Posts (www.geniushour.com/genius-hour-blog-posts): A blog with ideas about getting started with and holding Genius Hour in a classroom

Genius Hour Ideas (www.geniushour.com/2013/03/31/genius-hour-ideas): A webpage listing topics to use for research during Genius Hour

glitch: A problem that arises when using technology

Global Classroom Project, the (https://theglobalclassroomproject.org): An organization that connects teachers and students to enable them to collaborate globally; student work, resources, and information are shared in a wiki and a blog

Global Education Conference (www.globaleducationconference.com): An online, free, and global virtual conference that occurs over several days once a year; attendees include teachers, students, and educational leaders

Global Math Task Twitter Challenge (http://gmttc.blogspot.com): An effort to bring together mathematics students around the world to solve mathematics challenges and share their answers on Twitter using the hashtag #gmttc

Global Read Aloud (https://theglobalreadaloud.com): A reading program that connects classrooms through common read alouds

Global SchoolNet (www.globalschoolnet.org): An organization that encourages worldwide, collaborative educational projects

Glogster (http://edu.glogster.com): A subscription website where students can make *Glogs*, or multimedia mashups, to create a final product

Gmail (https://mail.google.com): Google's email platform

Google (www.google.com): A search engine developed by Google

Google Advanced Search (www.google.com/advanced_search): A search tool within Google that allows you to focus your search terms for better results

Google Chrome Store (https://chrome.google.com/webstore/category/apps): A place to discover apps, games, extensions, and themes for Google Chrome

Google ChromeCast: A fast, high-resolution device for delivering streaming video

Google Classroom (https://classroom.google.com): A file management system with some features of an LMS that allows classrooms to share announcements and documents and conduct discussions

Google CS First (www.cs-first.com/en/home): A free coding site where teachers sign up for a course and receive all the necessary materials to run a club or class that guides students through tutorials to learn Scratch coding

Google Docs (https://docs.google.com): A word processing tool in Google Drive, a part of the G Suite for Education, for creating and editing documents independently or in collaborative groups; available to all teachers and students who are members of the Google domain through their school, often called a *Google School*

Google Drawings (https://drawings.google.com): A drawing app within G Suite for Education

Google Drive (www.google.com/drive): A cloud-based storage platform that can store and sync files across multiple devices using a single login

Google Expeditions (https://edu.google.com/expeditions): A virtual reality app that allows students to immerse themselves in experiences from around the world and beyond

Google for Education (www.google.com/intl/en_us/edu): An overarching term for all the Google products that a school system has available for staff and student use

Google Forms (www.google.com/intl/en_us/forms/about): A survey and form-making app within G Suite for Education

Google Hangouts (https://hangouts.google.com): A unified communications service that allows members to initiate and participate in text, voice, and video chats either one on one or in a group and that is built into Google+ and Gmail and is available as an app for Apple and Android devices

Google Images (https://images.google.com): An image search engine from Google

Google Keep (https://keep.google.com): A cloud-based tool for gathering and organizing notes, lists, and ideas and sharing them for online collaboration

Google Maps (https://maps.google.com): Part of Google that students can use to generate maps to support their learning

Google My Maps (www.google.com/maps/d): A Google service where students create their own maps and insert place markers with additional data about a topic

Google Photos (https://photos.google.com): A photo storage, organization, and editing website, formerly called Picasa

Google Play (https://play.google.com): An entertainment platform for Google; includes an app store for Android apps, music, books, movies and TV, and a newsstand

Google Sheets (https://docs.google.com/spreadsheets): A spreadsheet app within G Suite for Education that supports common spreadsheet functions such as data entry, sorting, number calculation, and chart creation

Google Sites (https://sites.google.com): A free website builder created by Google

Google Slides (www.google.com/slides/about): A web-based presentation creator available in G Suite for Education that allows users to insert images, text, charts, and videos, as well as modify transitions, layouts, and backgrounds

Google Slides Q&A (www.google.com/slides/about): An add-on for Google Slides that allows presenters to take questions from the audience; the presenter shares a code and the audience can submit questions, which the presenter can view and answer during or after the presentation.

Google Tango (https://get.google.com/tango): An augmented reality app from Google that superimposes images on top of reality

Google URL Shortener (https://goo.gl): A tool for shortening URLs on the web to make it easier for someone to reach a specific webpage as quickly as possible

Google+ (https://plus.google.com): A social network where users can connect over a variety of interests; many educators post ideas, questions, and requests to connect with other classrooms through Skype, Google Hangouts, and blogging

Google+ Collections (https://plus.google.com/collections/featured): Allows users to group posts pertaining to a particular topic, providing an easy way to organize and share information

Google+ Communities (http://plus.google.com/communities): A social networking community where educators can connect by posting ideas, questions, and requests to connect with other classrooms through Skype, Google Hangouts, and blogs

Google+ Connected Classrooms Workshop (https://plus.google.com/communities /100662407427957932931): A Google+ community focused on bringing together educators from around the world to share ideas, collaborate, and discuss how to best use technology in the classroom

GoSoapBox (www.gosoapbox.com): A website that allows students to use digital clickers to respond to teacher-created questions

Green Screen (www.doink.com): An iOS app from Do Ink that makes it easy to use green screen effects to create movies

Haiku Deck (www.haikudeck.com): An online presentation tool for creating slides with beautiful images and limited text that includes a few free features and a premium version

hashtag: A type of label or metadata tag used on social network and microblogging services that makes it easier for users to find messages

Hour of Code (https://code.org/learn): An international event to encourage students of all ages to try coding; schools, public libraries, and community organizations hold programs where participants can try their hand at website-building, game creation, graphic design, and more

hyperdoc: A digital document that contains links to various online resources to save time as students quickly navigate to predetermined links and that teachers can share with students on the class LMS as active, clickable links

i-nigma (www.i-nigma.com/i-nigmahp.html): A QR code scanner website

iBooks Author (www.apple.com/ibooks): An Apple iOS and MacOS tool for creating an interactive book that is publishable in the iBooks Store; teachers need a teacher or district account to publish

iMovie (www.apple.com/imovie): An Apple video-creation app only available on an iPhone, an iPad, or a Mac computer

Infobase Learning (http://online.infobase.com/HRC/Browse/Product/8): An online database with videos and primary documents for student use

Infogram (https://infogram): A website with free and premium features for creating infographics using the data students collect

Infotopia (www.infotopia.info): A safe search engine for students

Instagram (www.instagram.com): A social media network for people to connect with others predominantly through pictures with short captions

interactive whiteboard: An interactive display board, often referred to as a *SMART Board* even though many different manufacturers exist, including SMART Technologies, Promethean, and Mimio

Internet Live Stats (www.internetlivestats.com): A site for monitoring how many users are using the Internet

iTunes (www.apple.com/itunes): Apple's media management program, available on MacOS and Windows personal computers, for users to download or publish their own music, videos, books, podcasts, and more

iWriteWords (https://itunes.apple.com/us/app/iwritewords-handwriting-game /id307025309?mt=8): A simple letter-tracing app

Jumpshare (https://jumpshare.com): A free service for storing and sharing photos, documents, and videos

Kahoot! (https://getkahoot.com): A free website for creating quizzes and answering the questions from any digital device

Kevin Honeycutt (http://kevinhoneycutt.org): A site with online collaborative projects created by educator Kevin Honeycutt, with many PBL opportunities for students and tool ideas to spark student and teacher creativity

Keynote (www.apple.com/keynote): An Apple presentation tool

Khan Academy (www.khanacademy.org): A screencast tutorial website for students to watch videos and check their understanding of concepts

Kidblog (https://kidblog.org): A website where students can publish and share their learning in a secure environment

Kiddle (www.kiddle.co): A visual search engine for students

KidRex (www.kidrex.org): An age-appropriate search engine for students

Kidtopia (www.kidtopia.info): A safe, custom Google search engine for elementary students

KidzSearch (www.kidzsearch.com): An age-appropriate search engine for students

Kinder Art (www.kinderart.com/arthistory): An age-appropriate site students can use to research the history of art

Kizoa (www.kizoa.com/School): A website for creating multimedia movies with images and music

Kodable (www.kodable.com): a free and paid website with a programming curriculum

KWL: A type of graphic organizer designed to help students learn by asking them the following questions: What do we know about this already? What do we want to know about this? What did we learn about this?

LastPass (www.lastpass.com): A secure password-creation and -management tool with free and paid versions

learning goal: An expectation and target for what students should learn and know

learning management system (LMS): Software used to manage, track, and report educational data and courses

Lego Mindstorms (www.lego.com/en-us/mindstorms): Lego kits with pieces that students can assemble into programmable robots

Library of Congress (www.loc.gov): The main research arm of the U.S. Congress, filled with collections of resources grouping primary source documents of all types

Life of Pix (www.lifeofpix.com): A free high-resolution photography resource for students to use and share

Lightbot (http://lightbot.com): An introductory coding website and app

LINER (http://getliner.com): An extension available for most web browsers that allows users to read, highlight, and share across different websites to help students organize research

Lino (http://en.linoit.com): A website of digital sticky notes for sharing memos, ideas, lists, photos, and so on

Listenwise (https://listenwise.com): A website that features new and academic stories that students can listen to

LogMeOnce (www.logmeonce.com): A website that allows users to create one secure password to access other websites where users have password-protected accounts

Lucidpress (www.lucidpress.com): A website where students and teachers can create stunning brochures, flyers, digital magazines, newsletters, and reports, with nothing to install on any device and the capability to add all types of media to a project with a simple drag-and-drop interface

Magic Move: A feature in Apple's Keynote presentation maker that can be inserted between two slides to make objects look like they are moving, such as the Earth rotating or ice melting

Magisto (www.magisto.com): A website and an app available for Apple and Android that turns video and images into movies

Make Art (https://art.kano.me/challenges): A coding website with tutorials to teach the user how to code and create artwork

Math Playground (www.mathplayground.com/mathprogramming.html): A website filled with mathematics resources and coding activities and games

Medium (https://medium.com): A platform where users can write, follow, and comment on blog posts written by writers from around the world

Microsoft Educator Community (https://education.microsoft.com): A Microsoft-run centralized website that pulls together lesson plans, technology integration ideas, opportunities for educators to collaborate, and much more

Microsoft Excel (https://products.office.com/en-us/excel): A spreadsheet program that you can use on both Apple and Windows devices and that makes up part of the Microsoft Office suite

Microsoft Office (https://products.office.com/en-US): A suite of software that contains Word, PowerPoint, Excel, and other Microsoft programs

Microsoft OneDrive (https://onedrive.live.com): A cloud-based data-storage platform where users can access their files from anywhere in the world

Microsoft OneNote (www.onenote.com): A digital notebook platform

Mimio (www.mimio.com/en-AP.aspx): One brand of interactive whiteboards and software solutions

Moodle (https://moodle.org): A free, open-source learning management system

Mozilla Firefox (www.mozilla.org/en-US/firefox/new): A web browser the global nonprofit company Mozilla created

My Storybook (www.mystorybook.com): A simple book-creation website

myON (www.myon.com): A reading platform based on student interest, reading level, and ratings of books

Mystery Skype (https://education.microsoft.com/skype-in-the-classroom /mystery-skype): A service offered on the Skype website to help teachers connect and collaborate with another unknown classroom

National Geographic (www.nationalgeographic.com): Houses a collection of information about geography, cartography, and exploration

National Geographic Kids (http://kids.nationalgeographic.com): A kid-friendly version of National Geographic with a collection of information and games

Nearpod (https://nearpod.com): A free and paid interactive presentation and lesson tool designed for teachers to embed questions, polls, and activities into presentations; teachers can access previously uploaded presentations through the website

NetSmartz (www.netsmartz.org): A website with resources teachers can use to support digital citizenship education in the classroom

Newsela (https://newsela.com): A site with leveled news, primary sources, standards-aligned formative assessments, and more that includes free content and premium features

NoodleTools (www.noodletools.com): An online research-management platform that promotes critical thinking and authentic research, helps students stay organized as they evaluate information and prepare to write, and allows librarians and teachers to provide feedback, monitor individual contributions to group work, and view statistics about source use

Notes: A default iOS app that allows users to take and share notes

NOW Classrooms Project, The (http://nowclassrooms.com/about): A website about the entire NOW Classrooms Project, including the *NOW Classrooms* blog and details about the book series

NSTeens (www.nsteens.org): A version of NetSmartz built specifically for teen users

Numbers (www.apple.com/numbers): Apple's iOS and MacOS spreadsheet tool that supports charts, tables, and images and provides a number of calculation and data-analysis tools

Otus (http://otus.com): A classroom LMS that integrates data from third parties to get a more comprehensive snapshot about student growth

Ozobot (www.ozobot.com): Small coding robots that help teach students how to code

Padlet (https://padlet.com): A digital bulletin board for student collaborative projects that students join through a code the teacher provides

Paint (http://microsoft_paint.en.downloadastro.com): A Microsoft tool for creating digital drawings that PC operating systems include

Pear Deck (www.peardeck.com): An interactive presentation platform where teachers can give various types of questions and get real-time feedback from students; Pear Deck presentations can be made from scratch on the website or uploaded from PowerPoint or a PDF

Pearson SuccessNet (www.pearsonsuccessnet.com): The online portal for many of Pearson's digital content solutions

PebbleGo (www.pebblego.com): A series of databases for beginning researchers enriched with audio and video media

Periscope (www.periscope.tv): A free app for livestreaming events on Twitter

Pexels (www.pexels.com): A free website students can use to access stock photos

Photos for Class (www.photosforclass.com): A collection of safe, attributed photos that creators license under Creative Commons for public use

Photoshop (www.adobe.com/photoshop): An image-editing program that can be accessed through the Adobe Creative Cloud for a monthly fee

PicCollage (https://pic-collage.com): A free media mashup app (with in-app purchases) for all devices that allows students to add pictures, stickers, and backgrounds and use various templates

PicMonkey (www.picmonkey.com): A free online image editor

Pics4Learning (www.pics4learning.com): A safe, free image library for educational use

Piktochart (https://piktochart.com): A template-driven website with free and premium features for easily creating stunning infographics

Pinterest (www.pinterest.com): A digital, visual bulletin board with ideas and links to a variety of teaching and learning ideas

Pixabay (https://pixabay.com): An international website for sharing high-quality public domain photos, illustrations, vector graphics, and film footage

Pixel Press (www.projectpixelpress.com): A tool used to learn coding and programming

Pixlr (https://pixlr.com/editor): A website used to edit images for free

Planet Nutshell (http://planetnutshell.com): A company whose primary focus is creating videos for businesses and free videos for teachers with resources on cyberbullying and Internet safety

PlayPosit (www.playposit.com): A free interactive website that allows teachers to post instructional videos while embedding questions throughout to receive feedback and give immediate feedback to their students on a lesson

Plickers (https://plickers.com): A website and a free app for Apple and Android devices that teachers can use to conduct quick formative assessments by scanning students' multiple-choice response codes in real time

Pocket (https://getpocket.com): A platform where users can save media they encounter online for later viewing

Podbean (www.podbean.com): A podcasting platform with both free and paid features

podcast: A digital audio recording that creators usually publish as a series of episodes

Pokémon Go (www.pokemongo.com): An augmented-reality app that encourages users to search for and collect virtual Pokémon in the real world

Poll Everywhere (www.polleverywhere.com): A survey platform where users can conduct various types of polls in real time, making the tool ideal for lessons, presentations, and real-time feedback; participants respond using any mobile phone that has texting capabilities

PowerPoint (https://products.office.com/en-us/powerpoint): Part of the Microsoft Office suite as well as the online Microsoft Office 365 subscription, which you can use on both Apple and Windows devices to create presentations

PowerSchool Learning (formerly Haiku Learning) (www.powerschool.com /solutions/lms): A learning management system with limited free access as well as premium features

Prezi (https://prezi.com): An online presentation-creation tool

Projects by Jen (https://projectsbyjen.com): A site with different online collaborative projects created by educator Jen Wagner that teachers can join

Promethean (www.prometheanworld.com): One brand of interactive whiteboards and software solutions

Publisher (https://products.office.com/en-us/publisher): Part of the Microsoft Office suite as well as the online Microsoft Office 365 subscription, which you can use on both Apple and Windows devices, with templates to create things like newsletters, posters, and other digital content

Puzzlets (www.digitaldreamlabs.com): A coding game by Digital Dream Labs that uses a puzzle board and puzzle pieces to help students learn how to code

QR code: A scannable code that links to online information

QR Reader (https://itunes.apple.com/us/app/qr-reader-for-iphone/id368494609 ?mt=8): A free QR code reader for the iPhone

QuickTime (https://support.apple.com/quicktime): A multimedia video player for mobile devices and personal computers that also allows for movie, screen, and audio recording

QuickVoice (www.nfinityinc.com/quickvoiceip.html): A voice recorder for iOS devices

Quizizz (https://quizizz.com): A free website for creating and storing quizzes that has leaderboards, music, and more to engage learners

random password generator: An app, website, or device for creating and storing strong user passwords; random password generators are a great way to introduce students to the idea of using safe passwords

Raspberry Pi (www.raspberrypi.org): A small, affordable computer that users can program in a variety of ways

Raz-Kids (www.raz-kids.com): A digital guided-reading program that provides teachers with digital, downloadable, and printable books

ReadWriteThink (www.readwritethink.org): A website that has many helpful tools for writing

Recap (https://letsrecap.com): An app that works on all devices that allows users to create videos with narration

Reflector (www.airsquirrels.com/reflector): A wireless receiver for mirroring and streaming content to and from devices

Remind (www.remind.com): A website that allows users to send messages to other users' devices

Reminders: A default iOS app that allows users to make a list of reminders

Roboblockly (http://roboblockly.ucdavis.edu): A digital, programmable robot focused on teaching coding and mathematics skills to elementary and middle school students

RUS evaluation questions: Questions designed to get students thinking about the reliability, usefulness, and scholarliness of every source they encounter

Safari (www.apple.com/safari): A web browser Apple developed that can only be used on Mac operating systems

Safe Kids (www.safekids.com): A free website filled with digital citizenship resources

Safe Search Kids (www.safesearchkids.com): A search engine for students

Safe Share (https://safeshare.tv): A free website that removes excess and distracting content, comments, or advertisements so that you can share videos with students

Safe YouTube (http://safeyoutube.net): A free website that allows users to import video links from other websites

SAMR model: A model that helps teachers to determine ways to increase effective use of technology in lessons; SAMR stands for *substitution, argumentation, modification,* and *redefinition*

sandbox: A term for a virtual space in which learners can securely play with and explore new or untested software without judgment

sandbox time: A time period, usually ten to fifteen minutes, that teachers designate for students to try out a new technology platform or for teachers to receive training on new technology

Scan (www.scan.me): A QR code generator and reader

Scholastic News (http://magazines.scholastic.com): An online, age-appropriate news site for students, organized and published by Scholastic, offering free stories as well as a paid classroom subscription

Scholastic Story Starters (www.scholastic.com/teachers/story-starters): A website where teachers can have students build stories

Schoolkit Math (www.schoolkitapps.com): An app that provides virtual mathematics manipulatives

Schoology (www.schoology.com): A learning management system containing a discussion board where students can write posts in response to an ongoing discussion

SchoolTube (www.schooltube.com): A source of videos specifically compiled for teachers and students

Scratch (https://scratch.mit.edu): A free coding language and online community developed by MIT that acts as the basis for Google CS First courses and tutorials

ScratchJr (www.scratchjr.org): A tool for learning a programming language

screencast: A recording of a digital screen with audio added to explain a concept

Screencastify (www.screencastify.com): An extension of the Chrome browser, or an application that users can install and run through the Chrome browser, used to create screencast movies

Screencast-O-Matic (https://screencast-o-matic.com): A free website with an inexpensive pro upgrade that teachers and students can use to create screencasts

screenshot: An image of the display on a computer screen

Scrible (www.scrible.com): A web-based tool for users to annotate PDFs, websites, and documents, including highlighting, adding electronic sticky notes, and underlining

Seesaw (http://web.seesaw.me): A site and app for creating student-driven digital portfolios, with free basic features, premium advanced features, and school versions

Shadow Puppet Edu (http://get-puppet.co): An app that allows students to make simple video slide shows

Showbie (www.showbie.com): A learning management system used to give and receive assignments while allowing for feedback

SimpleK12 (www.simplek12.com): A source for professional development for teachers

sketchnoting: A term for taking notes as a visual story with words and pictures to connect and communicate new ideas (visit Sketchnote Army [http://sketchnotearmy .com] to see examples)

SketchUp (www.sketchup.com): A tool used to model in 3-D that includes free and premium features

Skitch (https://evernote.com/products/skitch): An app that allows users to take and annotate pictures

Skype (www.skype.com/en): A video and instant messaging app that you can install on any type of device to collaborate with other classes and all types of experts

Skype in the Classroom (https://education.microsoft.com/skype-in-the-classroom/overview): An online community where teachers can find resources to use Skype in their classrooms, including information on guest speakers, Mystery Skype, virtual field trips, and lesson plans

SMART Technologies (https://home.smarttech.com): One brand of interactive whiteboards and software solutions

Smithsonian Institution (www.si.edu): The primary website for all of the Smithsonian museums

Smithsonian Learning Lab (https://learninglab.si.edu): A database of information for students to use as they research topics

Smithsonian Magazine (www.smithsonianmag.com): The magazine about the Smithsonian museums

Snapchat (www.snapchat.com): An image-messaging and multimedia social networking app, for users ages 13 and older, where students can create stories and share them with their followers

Snopes (www.snopes.com): A fact-checking website

Socratic seminars: A teaching method in which students help one another understand the ideas, issues, and values reflected in a specific text

Socrative (www.socrative.com): A tool to survey and assess progress that includes free and premium features

SoundCloud (https://soundcloud.com/mobile): A streaming site that provides access to music and allows users to upload their own

Soundtrap (www.soundtrap.com): A platform where users can digitally collaborate, create, store, and share music and podcasts

Sphero (www.sphero.com): A robotic toy that users can code using a corresponding app

Spreaker (www.spreaker.com): A platform for creating podcasts

StarBoards (www.touchboards.com/hitachi): An interactive whiteboard

Stickies (www.zhornsoftware.co.uk/stickies): A website that provides a downloadable program for using digital sticky notes on a PC

Sticky (www.stickynotesapp.com): An iOS app that mimics sticky notes on the screen

Stop Motion Studio (www.cateater.com/stopmotionstudio): A free app for creating stop-motion videos

Stormboard (https://stormboard.com): A collaborative online brainstorming environment students can access from any device

Storybird (www.storybird.com): A free story-creation website and app where users can choose art from professional artists to include as visual enhancements to their writing; users can publish, share, or purchase as a bound book finished stories on the site

SurveyMonkey (www.surveymonkey.com): A website with free and premium features for creating and circulating surveys

Swift Playgrounds (https://developer.apple.com/swift/playgrounds): An iPad-only app for learning Swift code in a fun, interactive way to help students understand app creation

Symbaloo (www.symbaloo.com): A social bookmarking website to organize research tools for students to access that works similarly to a hyperdoc but has much more visual appeal

Tackk (https://tackk.com): A free basic and easy-to-use electronic publishing site that lets users insert images, text, and videos and share their final product

Tangram Free (https://itunes.apple.com/us/app/tangram-free/id400629406?mt=8): A mathematics app that uses tangram shapes

TeacherTube (www.teachertube.com): A site for teachers and students to share instructional videos and other educational content

Teaching Channel (www.teachingchannel.org): An online community where teachers can watch videos and connect with other teachers about strategies to help students

tech-spert: An expert in a certain technology task, website, or application

TED-Ed lessons (https://ed.ted.com): A series of short animated videos accompanied with review questions, additional resources, and discussion questions created by animators at TED-Ed; an affiliation of TED

Tellagami (https://tellagami.com): An Apple-only app where students create an avatar, record a sound clip, and have a character play back the recording with added gestures

Tes Teach with Blendspace (www.tes.com/lessons): A tool that allows teachers to create a series of activities (like videos, quizzes, files, websites, and so on) that students can move through in order

ThemeSpark (www.themespark.net): A website for creating rubrics for projects

Thinglink (www.thinglink.com): A website with free and premium features for annotating images to demonstrate learning

TinyURL (https://tinyurl.com): A URL shortener that makes smaller, more manageable website addresses for student use

TodaysMeet (https://todaysmeet.com): A tool that provides a backchannel for participants to comment and provide input without disrupting a presentation

Tony Vincent Storyboards (http://learninginhand.com/blog/2014/8/6/plan-a -better-imovie-trailer-with-these-pdfs): A collection of storyboard templates that mirror iMovie trailers, allowing students to organize their ideas before they create a trailer

TouchCast (www.touchcast.com): A smart video-production website and app for both Apple and Android devices that allows students to create and share interactive videos

TPACK: Matthew Koehler's model for integrating Technological, Pedagogical, and Content Knowledge into teaching and learning

Trello (https://trello.com): A free website and app that allows students to create and organize lists within online boards; users can share Trello boards with each other, making task assignment and voting easy for group projects

Tumblr (www.tumblr.com): A platform where users can post, share, search for, and comment on a variety of media

TweenTribune (www.tweentribune.com): A Smithsonian site featuring free leveled news articles, primary sources, and quizzes

Tweetdeck (https://tweetdeck.twitter.com): an online tool for organizing Twitter lists and conversations

Twitter (https://twitter.com): A popular social media site for communicating short messages through text and multimedia; we encourage the use of a teacher or classroom account

Twitter Analytics (https://analytics.twitter.com): A Twitter tool for reviewing and analyzing activity on a twitter account

Twitter chats: A way for people in various types of communities to discuss ideas using specific hashtags

Tynker (www.tynker.com): A tool used to learn coding, which includes free and premium features

Typing Club (www.typingclub.com): A website that teaches typing

UJAM (www.ujam.com): An online audio mixer that allows users to record their voices and combine them with various music styles to create unique songs

unplugged coding: An activity one can conduct without the use of a computer or electronic equipment to understand how computer coding works

Unsplash (https://unsplash.com): A site for accessing Creative Commons–licensed photos

Video Star (http://videostarapp.com): A free app for iPads and iPhones designed to make music videos, with hundreds of built-in effects and filters

Vimeo (https://vimeo.com): A website where users over age thirteen can watch, upload, and share videos

virtual reality: A computer-generated version of reality that users can interact with using special equipment with built-in sensors, such as headsets or gloves

Voice Memos: An iOS app that allows you to record audio, edit your recorded audio, and export the file

VoiceThread (https://voicethread.com): A paid subscription website where teachers can set up an online collaborative space for students to create video, voice, and text commenting

Voxer (www.voxer.com): A website and iOS and Android app that allows individuals age thirteen and older to communicate with live audio feeds, voice recordings, written messages, or pictures

WatchKnowLearn (www.watchknowlearn.org): A website that contains free educational videos

Weebly (www.weebly.com): A template-based website builder with free and premium features

WeVideo (www.wevideo.com): A video-creation and video-sharing tool that uses cloud-based video-editing software and includes free and premium features

Wikimedia Commons (www.wikimedia.org): A collection of free-to-use media content; users may also upload and license their own works on Wikimedia Commons

Wikipedia (www.wikipedia.org): A free online encyclopedia that is open to users to add information (causing some to question its credibility as a primary research source) that is useful for finding additional sources of information

Wikispaces (www.wikispaces.com): An online collaboration platform that users can open or close to a global audience

Word (https://products.office.com/en-us/word): Part of the Microsoft Office suite as well as part of the online Microsoft Office 365 subscription that you can use on both Apple and Windows devices for word processing

Word Art (https://wordart.com): A tag cloud generator formerly called Tagul

Wordle (www.wordle.net): A tag cloud generator

WordPress (https://wordpress.com): A platform to create professional-looking blogs, websites, or portfolios that creators can maintain throughout their lives; WordPress software is free to use and it offers free site hosting

World Book Online (http://worldbookonline.com): An online encyclopedia, dictionary, and atlas

Writing Wizard (http://lescapadou.com): A tablet app that allows students to trace and learn letters, sight words, and teacher-created word lists; it is accessible through iTunes or the Google Playstore

Yahoo! (www.yahoo.com): A search engine developed by Yahoo!

YouTube (www.youtube.com): A video platform for publishing and viewing video content

YouTube Kids (https://kids.youtube.com): A student-friendly video-sharing app for finding and viewing student-safe videos

Zoom (https://zoom.us): A web- and video-conferencing platform

References and Resources

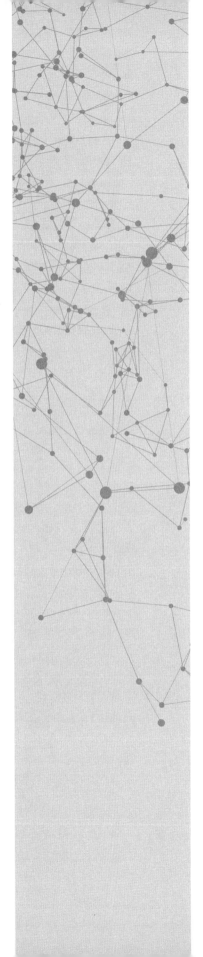

Azzam, A. M. (2014). Motivated to learn: A conversation with Daniel Pink. *Educational Leadership, 72*(1), 12–17.

Bebell, D., & Kay, R. (2010). One to one computing: A summary of the quantitative results from the Berkshire Wireless Learning Initiative. *Journal of Technology, Learning, and Assessment, 9*(2).

Bebell, D., & O'Dwyer, L. M. (2010). Educational outcomes and research from 1:1 computing settings. *Journal of Technology, Learning, and Assessment, 9*(1).

Belgrad, S., Burke, K., & Fogarty, R. (2008). *The portfolio connection: Student work linked to standards* (3rd ed.). Thousand Oaks, CA: Corwin Press.

Bellanca, J., & Brandt, R. (Eds.). (2010). *21st century skills: Rethinking how students learn.* Bloomington, IN: Solution Tree Press.

Bellanca, J., & Fogarty, R. (1991). *Blueprints for thinking in the cooperative classroom.* Palatine, IL: Skylight.

Bender, W. N. (2012). *Differentiating instruction for students with learning disabilities: New best practices for general and special educators* (3rd ed.). Thousand Oaks, CA: Corwin Press.

Bransford, J. D., Brown, A. L., & Cocking, R. R. (Eds.). (1999). *How people learn: Brain, mind, experience, and school.* Washington, DC: National Academy Press.

Brock, A., & Hundley, H. (2016). *The growth mindset coach: A teacher's month-by-month handbook for empowering students to achieve.* Berkeley, CA: Ulysses Press.

Brookhart, S. M. (2008). *How to give effective feedback to your students.* Alexandria, VA: Association for Supervision and Curriculum Development.

Brookhart, S. M. (2012). Preventing feedback fizzle. *Educational Leadership, 70*(1), 24–29.

Chapman, C. M., & King, R. S. (2009). *Differentiated instructional strategies for reading in the content areas* (2nd ed.). Thousand Oaks, CA: Corwin Press.

Chappuis, J. (2012). "How am I doing?" *Educational Leadership, 70*(1), 36–41.

Cornelius-White, J. H. D., & Harbaugh, A. P. (2010). *Learner-centered instruction: Building relationships for student success.* Thousand Oaks, CA: SAGE.

Costa, A. L. (2008). *The school as a home for the mind: Creating mindful curriculum, instruction, and dialogue* (2nd ed.). Thousand Oaks, CA: Corwin Press.

Drapeau, P. (2014). *Sparking student creativity: Practical ways to promote innovative thinking and problem solving.* Alexandria, VA: Association for Supervision and Curriculum Development.

DuFour, R., DuFour, R., & Eaker, R. (2008). *Revisiting Professional Learning Communities at Work: New insights for improving schools.* Bloomington, IN: Solution Tree Press.

DuFour, R., DuFour, R., Eaker, R., & Karhanek, G. (2010). *Raising the bar and closing the gap: Whatever it takes.* Bloomington, IN: Solution Tree Press.

Dweck, C. S. (2008). *Mindset: The new psychology of success.* New York: Ballantine Books.

Ferriter, W. M. (2014, November 11). *Are there WRONG ways to use technology?* [Blog post]. Accessed at www.solutiontree.com/blog/wrong-ways-to-use-technology/ on March 31, 2017.

Ferriter, W. M., & Garry, A. (2010). *Teaching the iGeneration: 5 Easy ways to introduce essential skills with web 2.0 tools.* Bloomington, IN: Solution Tree Press.

Ferriter, W. M., Ramsden, J. T., & Sheninger, E. C. (2011). *Communicating and connecting with social media.* Bloomington, IN: Solution Tree Press.

Fisher, D., & Frey, N. (2012). Making time for feedback. *Educational Leadership, 70*(1), 42–46.

Friedman, T. L. (2016). *Thank you for being late: An optimist's guide to thriving in the age of accelerations.* New York: Farrar, Straus and Giroux.

Fullan, M. (2008). *Six secrets of change: What the best leaders do to help their organizations survive and thrive.* San Francisco: Wiley.

Fullan, M., & Donnelly, K. (2013, July 16). *Alive in the swamp: Assessing digital innovations in education.* Accessed at www.nesta.org.uk/publications/alive-swamp -assessing-digital-innovations-education on March 31, 2017.

Fullan, M., & Langworthy, M. (2013). *Towards a new end: New pedagogies for deep learning.* Seattle, WA: Collaborative Impact.

Godin, S. (2008). *Tribes: We need you to lead us.* New York: Portfolio.

Gordon, J. (2007). *The energy bus: 10 rules to fuel your life, work, and team with positive energy.* Hoboken, NJ: Wiley.

Gregory, G. H. (2008). *Differentiated instructional strategies in practice: Training, implementation, and supervision* (2nd ed.). Thousand Oaks, CA: Corwin Press.

Gregory, G. H., & Chapman, C. M. (2013). *Differentiated instructional strategies: One size doesn't fit all* (3rd ed.). Thousand Oaks, CA: Corwin Press.

Gregory, G. H., & Kaufeldt, M. (2015). *The motivated brain: Improving student attention, engagement, and perseverance.* Alexandria, VA: Association for Supervision and Curriculum Development.

Gutierrez, K. (2016, June 21). *What are personal learning networks?* [Blog post]. Accessed at http://info.shiftelearning.com/blog/personal-learning-networks on July 20, 2017.

Hattie, J. (2012a). Know thy impact. *Educational Leadership, 70*(1), 18–23.

Hattie, J. (2012b). *Visible learning for teachers: Maximizing impact on learning.* London: Routledge.

Hattie, J. (2013). *Visible learning: A synthesis of over 800 meta-analyses relating to achievement.* London: Routledge.

Hord, S. M. (Ed.). (2004). *Learning together, leading together: Changing schools through professional learning communities.* New York: Teachers College Press.

International Society for Technology in Education. (n.d.). *National educational technology standards for teachers.* Accessed at https://www.iste.org/standards/standards/for-educators on July 20, 2017.

Jakes, D. (2016, July 12). *Educational ping pong* [Blog post]. Accessed at https://davidjakesdesigns.com/ideas/2016/7/12/educational-ping-pong on May 12, 2017.

Johnson, D. (2013). Technology skills every teacher needs. *Educational Leadership, 70*(6), 84–85.

Killion, J. (2011, September 1). *Theory of change and Common Core standards* [Blog post]. Accessed at http://blogs.edweek.org/edweek/learning_forwards_pd_watch/2011/09/common_core_standards_and_theory_of_change.html on January 10, 2017.

Mizell, H. (2010). *Why professional development matters.* Oxford, OH: Learning Forward. Accessed at https://learningforward.org/docs/pdf/why_pd_matters_web.pdf on January 10, 2017.

Munby, S., & Fullan, M. (2016). *Inside-out and downside-up: How leading from the middle has the power to transform education systems.* Reading, England: Education Development Trust. Accessed at http://michaelfullan.ca/wp-content/uploads/2016/06/EdDevTrust-Global-Dialogue-FINAL.pdf on March 31, 2017.

National School Public Relations Association. (2011). *National survey pinpoints communication preferences in school communication* [Press release]. Accessed at www.nspra.org/files/docs/Release%20on%20CAP%20Survey.pdf on March 31, 2017.

Partnership for 21st Century Learning. (2015). *The 4Cs research series.* Accessed at www.p21.org/our-work/4cs-research-series on March 8, 2017.

Pearlman, B. (2009). Making 21st century schools: Creating learner-centered schoolplaces/workplaces for a new culture of students at work. *Educational Technology, 49*(5), 14–19.

Pogrow, S. (2009). *Teaching content outrageously: How to captivate all students and accelerate learning, grades 4–12.* San Francisco: Jossey-Bass.

Puentedura, R. R. (n.d.). *Learning, technology, and the SAMR model: Goals, processes, and practice.* Accessed at www.hippasus.com/rrpweblog/archives/2014/06/29 /LearningTechnologySAMRModel.pdf on March 8, 2017.

Robinson, K. (2009). *The element: How finding your passion changes everything.* New York: Viking.

Schiller, S. Z. (2009). Practicing learner-centered teaching: Pedagogical design and assessment of a second life project. *Journal of Information Systems Education, 20*(3), 369–381.

Speck, M., & Knipe, C. (2001). *Why can't we get it right?: Professional development in our schools.* Thousand Oaks, CA: Corwin Press.

Sullo, B. (2007). *Activating the desire to learn.* Alexandria, VA: Association for Supervision and Curriculum Development.

Taranto, G., Dalbon, M., & Gaetano, J. (2011). Academic social networking brings Web 2.0 technologies to the middle grades. *Middle School Journal, 42*(5), 12–19.

Tate, M. L. (2010). *Worksheets don't grow dendrites: 20 instructional strategies that engage the brain* (2nd ed.). Thousand Oaks, CA: Corwin Press.

Tate, M. L. (2012). *"Sit and get" won't grow dendrites: 20 professional learning strategies that engage the adult brain* (2nd ed.). Thousand Oaks, CA: Corwin Press.

Tomlinson, C. A. (2003). *Fulfilling the promise of the differentiated classroom: Strategies and tools for responsive teaching.* Alexandria, VA: Association for Supervision and Curriculum Development.

Tomlinson, C. A., & McTighe, J. (2006). *Integrating differentiated instruction and understanding by design: Connecting content and kids.* Alexandria, VA: Association for Supervision and Curriculum Development.

Tovani, C. (2012). Feedback is a two-way street. *Educational Leadership, 70*(1), 48–51.

Visible Learning. (n.d.). *Hattie ranking: 195 influences and effect sizes related to student achievement.* Accessed at http://visible-learning.org/hattie-ranking-influences-effect -sizes-learning-achievement/ on December 3, 2013.

Wald, P. J., & Castleberry, M. S. (Eds.). (2000). *Educators as learners: Creating a professional learning community in your school.* Alexandria, VA: Association for Supervision and Curriculum Development.

Wiggins, G. (2012). Seven keys to effective feedback. *Educational Leadership, 70*(1), 10–16.

Wiliam, D. (2011). *Embedded formative assessment.* Bloomington, IN: Solution Tree Press.

Wiliam, D. (2012). Feedback: part of a system. *Educational Leadership, 70*(1), 30–34.

Index

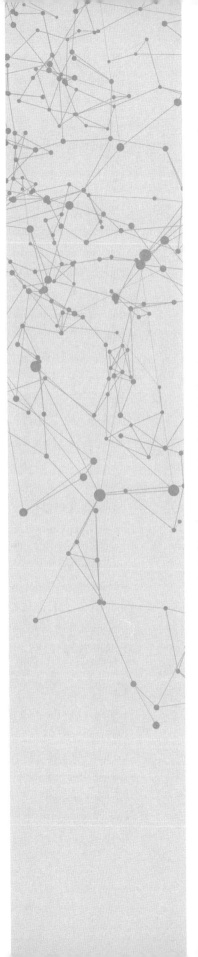

Now Classrooms Series
Meg Ormiston et al.

This practical series presents classroom-tested lessons that educators can rely on to engage students in active learning, critical thinking, and problem solving. Use these lessons to connect technology to key learning outcomes and prepare learners to succeed in the 21st century.

BKF797, BKF798, BKF799, BKF800, BKF801

Creating a Digital-Rich Classroom
Meg Ormiston

Design and deliver standards-based lessons in which technology plays an integral role. This book provides a research base and practical strategies for using web 2.0 tools to create engaging lessons that transform and enrich content.

BKF385

Designing Teacher-Student Partnership Classrooms
Meg Ormiston

Discover how teachers can become learning partners with their students. Cultivate a classroom environment in which students can apply what they've learned, teach it to their teacher and fellow students, and understand how their knowledge will be useful beyond the classroom.

BKF680

Create Future-Ready Classrooms, Now!
Meg Ormiston

Unite pedagogy and technology to inspire systemic school change. Explore digital tools that help seamlessly incorporate the technology-rich world into the classroom, understand how to use media for deeper learning, and examine a new approach to engagement and recognition.

BKF633

Solution Tree | Press a division of Solution Tree

Visit SolutionTree.com or call 800.733.6786 to order.

Wait! Your professional development journey doesn't have to end with the last pages of this book.

We realize improving student learning doesn't happen overnight. And your school or district shouldn't be left to puzzle out all the details of this process alone.

No matter where you are on the journey, we're committed to helping you get to the next stage.

Take advantage of everything from **custom workshops** to **keynote presentations** and **interactive web and video conferencing**. We can even help you develop an action plan tailored to fit your specific needs.

Let's get the conversation started.

Call 888.763.9045 today.

SolutionTree.com